# THE PRINCIPLES OF HIGHLY SUCCESSFUL NONPROFITS

How to Deliver Impact for your Beneficiaries and Increase Contributions

Mark Gruner

*This book is dedicated to my wife, family and friends for their support and understanding.*

*This book is also dedicated to my colleagues, staff, supervisors who were simply amazing to work with and accomplished so much, if you recognize yourself in some of these chapters, yes, that is you. Thanks!*

*Lastly, if there is something written about what not to do and you recognize yourself, yes, that is you! Take thanks that you are inspiring many on how not to do things. You're welcome.*

*"We make a living by what we get, we make a life by what we give."*

WINSTON CHURCHILL

# CONTENTS

# PREFACE

After working for some successful nonprofits and less success-ful to even struggling nonprofits, it is clear what distinguishes the highly successful from the others. The highly successful nonprofits follow some common sense principles that others do not. Many may follow a few but ignore other principles al-together and this is what makes the difference from struggling to highly successful. While some principles are followed some basic ones are not followed. Not every principle must be ad-hered to as there are compensating factors. However, when a nonprofit does not follow these principles and the factors that covered for these weaknesses no longer exist, this opens the door for chaos. Part of this challenge is due to the very nature of nonprofits, many will assume what works in for-profits will also work here, this is only true some of the time.

Whether you are a leader in a for-profit organization or a non-profit organization, it is critical to understand financial reports. As globalization expands there is more and more need to have a common understanding and a common way to interpret finan-cial statements. There is vast progress on this front with the advancement of International Financial Reporting Standards (IFRS) but there remains a long way to go.

The goal of this book is to assist leaders in understanding how nonprofits function best, which principles should be followed for success, what comprises good governance for both the profit organization and the nonprofit, as well to understand the rationale of accounting and financial statements with regards to both profit and nonprofit entities. How the standards are developed and why they are developed. How some countries developed their Generally Accepted Accounting Principles (GAAP) in many different ways from other countries. While at the same time, keeping some fundamental principles the same, such as the accrual basis of accounting which uses the matching principle for both revenues and expenses. This is the gold standard and accepted by the vast majority.

Any leader who is contemplating working at a nonprofit or who already does work at a nonprofit should understand these issues and understand how nonprofits work and what comprises good governance. When moving from a profit organization one may see a very different way that the nonprofit functions. The general reaction would be that they are doing something incorrectly. Many would think that we used to do it this way at our company, hence this nonprofit must be wrong. The truth of the matter is both can be correct. It is very important to understand that the goals and motivations of a nonprofit are very different from a for-profit company. This is usually the rationale for the very different way of operating, not that one is correct and the other wrong. It takes most people some time to understand this concept and the reason for this difference.

For those not working in a nonprofit environment, you will gain a better understanding of what makes a nonprofit tick and how these differences have an effect on the operations, the principles, and the financial reporting of the organization.

# INTRODUCTION

It was a few years after the devastating war across the country at that time known as Former Yugoslavia. I was now calling Sarajevo, Bosnia my home. I got to know the Bosnian people and felt they were a rightly proud people, but they came from a more complex background. I remember thinking that I used to think my background was complex, coming from Montreal, which can be torn between two languages. This was also a few years after the 1995 referendum in Quebec, so a very interesting time. Despite any differences between Anglophones and Francophones, there is still a strong bond between these two groups. I believed that the two groups make each other better. The combination of French and English make Montreal a great city. In Bosnia and the countries of Former Yugoslavia, the complexities are far greater and go back far more centuries. I will not even begin to try to explain the complexities.

I was starting a new job, I was the new Chief Financial Officer for the Commission for Real Property Claims of Displaced Persons and Refugees, (CRPC). CRPC was also known as Annex 7 of the Dayton Peace Agreement. This agreement was set up as a way to stop the fighting in the Balkans. Annex 7 was set up to determine the property rights of people that were forced to flee from their properties. Upon arriving to start on my first day, I met with my new team. I had one cashier, she was a nice lady with an interesting character, but not trained in accounting, but a very good cashier, nonetheless. My other staff member was a 19-year-old girl, who was entering the data, was bright, and had the potential to learn. I asked my team, which software are we using, they told me that they use excel. I asked for the list of financial policies, they informed me that there was none. I thought to myself, what have I gotten myself into here.

It was August when I started and on my first day, I realized that we did not have any of the tools that we would need to make a finance team functional. We did not have a reporting system, we did not have policies, we did not even have vouchers prepared. I looked at the calendar and realized that our annual audit would be starting in about six months. We would have to completely revamp this finance team to get it up to speed and operational. I met with the CEO, who was a great boss to have. He told me whatever I needed, he will provide. I explained, that we will need three things to start with. I will need to hire one or two more local staff, I would need to put in a financial reporting system, and I will need you and the board to approve the policies I put forward. He said, "Done, done and done."

With this vote of approval, I immediately went to look for two new staff to complement my team, I reviewed different accounting software packages, started preparing each policy, and prepared a voucher for us to use. I explained to my teams how to do bank reconciliations and cash reconciliations. We worked backward in time, from day one, about a year and a half before I joined. I was preparing for the possibility of missing thousands of dollars. Not because things were stolen but because people may forget to record a transaction or they would be lost. To my delight, after all the bank reconciliations were done there was only $46 missing. I told that to my boss Steve and he reached into his pocket and said, "I think I remember taking out $50, and perhaps they forgot to issue a receipt." He handed me the money and winked. We were both pleased that it was such a low amount.

The policies were unanimously approved and were being applied. People now had to get trips approved in advance and explain why they are traveling, rather than just writing, "Trip". These small changes led to great structural improvements in efficiency. The software package allowed me to report on various grants and prepare our financial statements, in a much more effective way than using excel could.

The audit was now a few weeks away, but we were now fully prepared, I had my team prepare all the working papers for them and had a review of them before submission. We submitted each bank and cash reconciliation to them and our fixed assets registry. Each donor agreement and receipt was prepared for them in a folder. The auditors arrived and did their work. They came to our office smiling each day. As is customary, on the final day, my team took them out to dinner. The manager of their team told me, "Mark, not sure what you did but we do not recognize your company, last year the systems were so bad, we almost issued a denial of opinion. This year you are one of our best-managed companies. I see you started six months ago, going from worst to best, great job.

The reality is that it would be wrong to take the credit for this. The main person that allowed for this success was Steven Segal (not the actor), who without his trust and support, none of this would have been possible. I did my job, what he did was take a risk.

There was a financial cost for those changes. The software package cost about $30 K, the two new staff another $30 K, but we had a much better operational organization. We saved tens of thousands of dollars in expenses and most importantly, with our stronger financial controls in place, our donor contributions increased by 50% within one year after these changes.

I learned two things from this experience, that success comes from hard work, but also in getting the right person to believe in you. This also taught me the critical relationship that must exist between a CEO and a CFO for success to exist.

Throughout my career, I have learned what makes a nonprofit successful and also what makes a nonprofit less successful. Interestingly, these principles should be known by most, but they are not always followed and sometimes completely ignored. It is also important to realize that small changes in the right direction can result in huge improvements, the same is true for small changes in the wrong direction. The goal of this book is to help to ensure that the small changes we make are in the correct direction.

Some chapters may get into some financial details, please do not get bogged down by this, continue reading, it will make sense later. Out of twenty chapters there are about four that are related to financial matters. As this topic is also critical to success, I could not leave it out.

# CHAPTER 1 -
# THE GOOD

T he impact that the nonprofit delivers is one of the strongest principles for success. For the nonprofit to succeed they must be able to deliver powerful impact at a reasonable cost. This will make their projects very effective and sought after by donors. The impact that they deliver must be relevant and seen as desirable among the international and donor community.

"THE IMPORTANT WORK OF MOVING THE WORLD FORWARD
DOES NOT WAIT TO BE DONE BY PERFECT MEN." - GEORGE ELIOT

**What is a nonprofit?**
A nonprofit or nonprofit organization (NPO) is a legal structure, it could be incorporated, a partnership or a trust that has a purpose and that is to deliver some positive impact. This could be in the form of reducing poverty, reducing hunger, reducing disease, helping social justice, reducing gender inequality and many more potential positive impacts, their goal is to make the world better by focusing on their mandate.

When we think about how our society functions we have two main sectors, there is the public sector, this is the government and we have the private sector, this is the sector where the for-profit companies occupy, such as Coke, McDonald's and many others. The balance between the public sector and the private sector is determined by the Country in which you live. The more the balance is towards the private sector, the more capitalistic is the society, such as the United States. The more balanced towards the public sector, the country would be more socialistic. If the balance is more towards the private sector, one could say it is right-leaning and if more balanced towards the public, it would be left-leaning.

The nonprofits fall outside of both of these sectors and form a third sector or the nonprofit sector. They generally try to improve society and sometimes fill in where the public sector has not been able to produce results or on areas that are not the focus of the public sector. These nonprofits are funded through a multitude of donors, many contributions come from the public, but also the private and public sector.

Many potential impacts are highly relevant, the very common ones are fighting against poverty, hunger, diseases, others include working on building better educational systems, improving gender equality, improving clean water and a host of many others. There are seventeen United Nations Sustainable Development Goals. Almost two hundred countries agreed that the focus on these seventeen goals would help make the world better. It is critical that the successful nonprofit works in one or many of these goals. The first two are poverty and hunger. If a nonprofit aligns its priorities with these goals, then they will align with the vast majority of donors and their impact will be relevant. The next step will be the ability to deliver on those priorities.

**Success Indicators**

A nonprofit organization and a for-profit company are very different. When we look at success in a company, it is relatively easy to determine. Are they making a profit or not? This may not be the only thing to look at but it is a critical thing to look at and ultimately if a company cannot create a profit, they will not be in business too long. With the nonprofit, there is not an uncomplicated way to measure success. One may look at whether they have a surplus or a deficit in the year. This gives a little understanding, but it is not a significant factor to determine success. The nonprofit may increase the number of new projects they have and incurring unfunded costs to do so, that would lead to a potential deficit in the year. The reason they may do this is they understand that this will lead to increased results for their beneficiaries and then ultimately lead to an increase in donor contributions. Here, using the Profit & Loss (P&L) Statement as a gauge for success will lead to incorrect conclusions in the nonprofit environment. The P&L equivalence is called the Statement of Activities. Technically the nonprofit does not have profits or losses, but they have surpluses and deficits. By using the Statement of Activities it would be very difficult to determine whether a nonprofit is successful.

A better gauge would be to look at the Balance Sheet or the equivalent in the nonprofit environment would be the Statement of Financial Position. One could review the reserves or the net assets. The net assets is like equity in the for-profit company. In a company, we divide the balance sheet between Assets, Liabilities, and Equity, with the formula A= L+E, while in the nonprofit, the formula is A=L+N (N is for net assets). There are no owners or shareholders in a nonprofit, hence, the terminology must change. The amount of net assets as compared to the annual spend can be seen as a gauge of sustainability, which would be one way to determine success. However, the net assets could have been built up over many decades and recent years could show another reality.

Since there is no straightforward way to tell whether a nonprofit is successful, but we know that a nonprofit that can deliver strong results at a reasonable cost will be highly successful, therefore, we should use that as a gauge to determine their success today. While this is true, there is no financial report that states this. There are Metrics and Evaluation (M&E) reports and as well as financial reports, but there is not one that determines whether a nonprofit is efficient at achieving results. The only way to see this success or lack of success is by looking at what occurs with highly effective and successful nonprofits. They are highly sought after by donors and this efficiency will translate to an increase in donor revenues. Hence, a nonprofit that improves their effectiveness at delivering results for their intended beneficiaries will also see an increase in funding from donors. Similarly, a nonprofit that is becoming less efficient in the ability to drive results will see a decline in funding from donors. Many other factors will play a role whether the funding increases or decreases such as geopolitical events, a depressed global economy, a change in priorities for the donor community and others, but mostly where there is no clear explanation for the rise or fall of donor funding, it is likely tied to this factor.

Hence, all things being equal, an improvement in efficiency will increase funding and a decrease in efficiency will cause less funding. Therefore, one way to measure the success of a nonprofit or lack of success would be the changes in funding from donors. It is important to note that funding is very different from revenue. The revenues can be realized in one year from a grant agreement signed four years ago. The real gauge for success would be the volume of newly signed grants as compared with the most recent years average. A decline would show that the nonprofit is becoming less relevant and that is being reflected by fewer donors funding that nonprofit.

One may conclude that the most important principle is to generate donor agreements and there is some truth to that, however, to increase donor contributions the nonprofit must be able to generate impact for its beneficiaries. They will see those nonprofits with a history of being able to generate results that are effective and improve the lives of their beneficiaries as more desirable to work with compared to those nonprofits that cannot generate such results as efficiently.

Being able to drive more donor contributions may be seen as a principle for success, but this way of thinking is incorrect. It is a sign of success not a principle of success. By being successful, the nonprofit will have increased contributions, which is the result of success not the cause of success. The success is the ability to drive strong results at an efficient cost, this success will lead to an increase in donors wanting to partner with a successful nonprofit. Many nonprofits do not understand this properly and focus more attention on fundraising than on being effective at delivering results. This is not to say that no efforts should be spent on fundraising, but you must first have a strong product before you can sell it.

## Success Factors

Many factors contribute to whether a nonprofit can generate positive results for its beneficiaries efficiently, but the most important would be the management team, especially the CEO and the Board. A CEO will either have a positive effect regarding this efficiency or a negative effect. The CEO who has a positive effect on this will see the donor contributions rise and will see the nonprofit increase it's standing in the international community, it will also see an increase in sustainability or its financial health. A CEO that harms efficiency will see donor contributions become decreased and the standing in the international community will also diminish. The Board is there to ensure that if there is a problem with the efficiency and the negative effects are starting to show, that they make appropriate changes to solve the issue.

One of the key principles for a successful nonprofit is the ability to deliver strong and relevant results for their intended beneficiaries at a reasonable cost. This will highlight to donors that they are a good investment and they will be that much more likely to contribute. The nonprofit that can achieve this principle will have a large competitive advantage over another that cannot.

How does one attain stronger results? Many factors play a role in this. The first is ensuring that the nonprofit focuses on relevant and efficient projects. It would make sense that only the best projects are maintained and efforts are made to increase or duplicate these projects, while less efficient projects are removed or improved so they now become efficient. If they cannot improve a project where it is efficient, they should remove it. A key factor is the staff that the nonprofit has and how the staff is motivated. A nonprofit could have the most talented staff around, but if they are not properly motivated to drive results, this will not yield significant results. The staff that a nonprofit has is tantamount to success, but the nonprofit must be able to motivate them and maintain them. This comes from the top. The CEO is critical to ensure that they do this correctly. Hence, the CEO will have a significant impact on whether the nonprofit is successful.

# CHAPTER 2 -
# PROJECTS

T hese are key components of any nonprofit. For the most part, if you do not have projects then you do not have an NPO.

**Projects**

Projects can be defined as those undertakings or activities which together form to generate a positive result or outcomes and impact. In short, projects use resources and deliver results. An efficient project is one that uses resources with very little waste and delivers positive outcomes. An effective project is a project that delivers results efficiently and those results have a positive effect or impact. One can also view a highly efficient project as one that delivers significant outcomes and impacts but spends little resources. Hence, projects that have a high value of results compared to the value of resources consumed would be highly successful projects. A basic principle for success in the nonprofit world would be to be able to regularly deliver highly efficient projects. This will be a significant help to your beneficiaries and your projects will be sought after by donors.

One could consider a nonprofit to be the sum total of its projects and then add in the admin side or the non-project side. Hence, in many cases the projects would form approximately

85% of the nonprofit costs and the remaining 15% would be considered admin costs or non-project costs. These ratios can vary slightly and can vary on how one defines a project cost versus a non-project cost or an admin cost versus a project cost. The past history of the nonprofit would be an indication of what you could potentially achieve and your most recent history would be of higher significance.

Another way to look at projects in a nonprofit is by looking at the construction of a house, the projects would be the bricks of the house, a critical component, while the administration side would be the cement, that holds the bricks together. This can also be similar to looking at the bricks as your restricted grants and your unrestricted grants or earned revenue as your cement, both of these analogies are quite similar and a good way of understanding project costs and non-project costs. One important distinction is that the earned revenue and unrestricted projects often fund projects and not only admin costs. However, without unrestricted funds or unearned revenue, it will make building the nonprofit much more challenging.

## Admin Costs versus Project Costs

Some argue that the admin cost and non-project costs are the same, but some can define a project cost as any cost that is funded by a project. With this definition, what occurs when an admin cost is funded by a donor or project? Using that definition a cost that by nature is an admin cost now becomes a project cost. Hence, for the purpose of this book, we argue that the funding source should not determine whether an expense is project in nature or admin in nature. The nature of the expense would determine the nature or classification of project and admin and not the source of funding. As such, it is possible to have admin costs that are funded by donors, as well, it is possible to have project costs that are not funded by donors. In essence, the source of funding plays no role in this determination.

There are many costs that are funded by donors that are truly project costs but there is also funding for admin costs. Hence project efficiency levels should compare how much funds actually go to the project and then the overall admin level of an entity.

This idea works when all entities use the same definition for admin costs and project costs, but what if some entities decide that certain admin costs are now project costs since they are funded by a donor. This would result in some entities overstating their project costs and understating their admin costs. Unfortunately, this occurs more frequently than one would anticipate. An entity can simply lower their admin cost by redefining what is an admin cost and what is not. This makes comparison across entities much more difficult. Having this approach may work for the entity to show a lower admin rate, but it will work against that same entity by having a higher project cost and the end result will be, projects that have the same results but have higher costs. Hence, it is important to consider all factors together and not have one factor play a more dominant role than the other. Unfortunately, it is very simple to move from a 25% admin rate to a 15% admin rate, you simply need to redefine what is an admin cost. Perhaps, by making one small change and ruling that any cost that is funded by a project or a donor, can no longer be an admin cost, this change alone could have a drastic effect on the admin rate of the entity. Our recommendation is to keep the definitions of admin costs and project costs separated from whether a cost is funded by a donor or not and stick to the sole nature of the expense.

**Redefining Admin Costs**

In the year an entity changes their definition of admin costs to exclude any admin costs that are funded by donors, the entity has not become any more efficient, even though it has improved its admin rate from 25% to 15%, it simply has moved some of the "inefficiency" to projects. While this ratio is important it is clearly more important to see how much value the project is estimated to deliver versus the cost. This should be the number one factor, and this should take into account the admin cost ratio. If an entity has a 50% admin rate, then they are clearly doing something wrong. They are likely understating the project costs to get a favorable result of costs versus results. Any NPO with such a high admin rate should be asked how they can remain competitive. The only possible way for them to be competitive would be that they have a significant amount of earned income or they have a significant sum of unrestricted funding, which they are defining as admin costs and not project costs.

Hence, the total costs play more of a role than the project costs alone, this will take into account those entities with a higher admin rate and compare it with those that have a lower admin rate. This may be very complex to achieve as most NPOs will have hundreds of projects and getting an estimate of the full amount of impact and outcomes will not be easy. As well, most of the impact and outcomes will be very different among the different projects.

This process and evaluation will never be perfect, but despite never being perfect it should be attempted. As well, it will demonstrate that one of the most critical factors in the success of an entity is the amount of trust that a given NPO can generate with their donors. The opposite is even more acute if donors lack trust in an NPO, they and others will be very reluctant to fund and this will likely result in the entity to collapse if some other donor does not come to its rescue or they do not make changes to restore any lack of trust.

The events can turn quite quickly, once an entity loses trust from donors, the immediate effect will be less funding. This will then have an effect of an increased admin rate and less time to devote to projects. Management will be forced to figure out what is going wrong. There will be increased demands on the finance teams and donor fundraising teams. These will provide little results as there is already a lack of trust which has not been addressed. Things will get worse as the admin costs are increasing as a ratio and more time is devoted to these efforts. The productivity of projects will decrease. This will drive even less funding. This could require more aggressive accounting techniques which could further reduce trust and create a catch-22 or a downward spiral.

Entities that are facing this situation would be wise to discuss with the donor teams and donors to find out what is occurring, it may even be wise to bring truly independent auditors to assist with what is going on. This will not be an easy fix, but ignoring the issue and hoping it goes away will result in a definite collapse of the entity within a few years.

**Project Life Cycle**

The project life cycle follows a very traditional path. Projects start their life out as a proposal. This would be a document that outlines what the project hopes to achieve and what the costs are and a narrative that explains the project in more detail. The three main components are the narrative, the expected M&E and the budget. This way a donor can then decide if this project is worth funding, does it meet their objectives, are the outcomes positive in view of the costs. If it meets these criteria, the proposal would be then discussed further and likely funded. At the time of signing, it now is a project and no longer a proposal. The project runs through its expected time and then closes, after the time the project has concluded or all the funds have been spent.

The project will have reporting requirements, they can be quarterly, semi-annually or annual reporting. With each report, the standard package would be a narrative report, an actual cost versus budget report and an M&E report showing actual results to date versus expected. This way the donor would be able to see how the project is doing both in terms of spending and in terms of achieving expected outcomes or results. The narrative will go to further explain the details. This will give the donor assurance that the project is on track or whether it is falling behind.

Finally, when the project is completed there will be a completion report, which will provide details of the full spend, the full delivery of outcomes and impacts and the narrative will explain any successes or failures of the project. This is an important report for any donor that is closing a project and will play an important role in any future funding from that donor.

These reports should be well prepared and reviewed by many individuals before sending out to the respective donor. Errors here could have a large effect on trust, as well any large discrepancy in delivery should be well explained and they should be reasonable.

# CHAPTER 3 - YIN AND YANG OF A NONPROFIT

"THE BEST WAY TO FIND YOURSELF IS TO LOSE YOURSELF IN THE SERVICE OF OTHERS." - MAHATMA GANDHI

E ach nonprofit must have an impact statement, what is their goal, what are they trying to achieve? In what way are they looking to improve in the world? Some NPOs may be fighting against poverty, hunger or fighting AIDS. There are hundreds of great causes out there and many nonprofits can help deliver great impact. They may fight for children or women or disadvantaged people, all of them are looking to make the world a better place. They are striving to deliver a positive impact. The focus on impact is a clear principle that can make a nonprofit highly successful. A nonprofit that can deliver strong results and impact is a necessary ingredient for success.

In addition to achieving a strong impact, each NPO must be sustainable, they must figure a way to create a reserve and to have earned income which can help their sustainability and overall going concern. If an NPO does not keep a focus on their sustainability, then they can find themselves going broke very soon and they would no longer be in a position to achieve the good that they hope to deliver. To achieve good sustainability many will earn interest revenue, earn dividends and earn gains on sales of securities. This may seem counterintuitive to many, as many may feel this should not be part of the normal operations of a nonprofit, but to remain solvent and be more effective, this is exactly what they should be doing. The focus of their work should be on delivering impact, but a small fraction of their time should be spent on ensuring the best return on their reserves and on building a significant sum of reserves.

## Impact and Sustainability

We can consider the impact as yin and sustainability as yang. While these two may seem like opposing forces, they are very complementary. One may hear, why is that NPO making money on selling investments, they should be putting that money to deliver impact. The reality is these earnings will go to delivering impact but at a time when it is needed. It is similar to saving for a rainy day. It is important to also note, that any investment income will only be made on the reserves that the NPO has built up and not on the donor's current contributions. NPOs may earn simple bank interest on donor funds, but the earnings are part of the donors' funds, not the NPO's. Rather than having these reserves sitting as cash in the bank, they will be better used by investing them and earning a strong return. This will create a stronger and more sustainable NPO. It will allow them more decision making power and the ability to ride out any droughts in donor funding. One can see that by focusing some efforts on sustainability, it actually has a positive effect on delivering impact.

Yin and yang is a well-known concept of dualism in ancient Chinese philosophy which depicts how what seems like opposing forces are actually complementary and interconnected in the natural world.

Any good nonprofit must have a strong yin and yang. In more

conventional terms the nonprofit must have strong sustainability and deliver strong impact. The impact can be considered the good that it does. Why is the world better by having this NPO? Does the NPO alleviate poverty in a given region, does it fight against hunger or does it fight diseases like malaria or AIDS? All of these and much more would be considered its impact or its doing good. Equally important is its sustainability. The sustainability is similar to a going concern but more long term in nature. It is the concept that the NPO will exist in the future. There are exceptions to this, such as entities that are set up with a fixed mandate and for a fixed period, but apart from these, the general idea is that the nonprofit will continue to operate into the foreseeable future.

### Should a Nonprofit focus on Sustainability

One may think that it is sufficient to have one or the other. For example, many from the public may say that an NPO should not think about its sustainability and only be concerned with its impact. The problem with this concept is that if an entity is not concerned with their sustainability then they will not exist for that long and the good that they are doing will no longer continue. On the other hand, if an entity is too concerned with its sustainability and loses sight of the good that it does or should do, this will also end in poor results. Since they are no longer concerned with delivering impact, their results will suffer and as a result, their funding will drop. By not delivering results, this will negatively affect its sustainability. The reality is that by spending a small fraction of time on sustainability, one can achieve great results. It does not take that much time or effort to manage a strong portfolio, while maintaining strong results do require time and efforts.

The balance between sustainability and delivering strong results must always be in check. There are times where certain activities will primarily focus on delivering impact or on ensuring sustainability, this is fine and normal. However, on a whole every day and month, there should be a strong balance between the two. Hence, if a nonprofit has a surplus balance of $50 M, there is no issue with putting those funds in an investment vehicle to drive up investment income and increase sustainability. This is fine and this would be a transaction that can be considered purely on the side of sustainability, however, the income derived from those investments should go to furthering the impact of the organization.

There may be years where the impact is more important than sustainability. This could occur when a tragic event occurs and there is not enough time to apply for additional funds, the entity may decide to use a part of their reserves to help those due to the disaster or crisis. There are other years where there are more favorable conditions and this could allow for an increase in surplus or sustainability. This can then be used later due to poorer conditions or a crisis such as a fire or a flood, such as the fires in Brazil and Australia during 2019.

## Balancing Yin and Yang

This balance is critical to have, an overall strong health, if an entity focuses too much on sustainability, they will lose sight of the real reason they exist in the first place and that is to achieve their goal which is to make the world a better place, by alleviating poverty, hunger, disease or another lofty goal. If this situation were to become persistent it could even have the public questioning their reason to exist. This would not be good and would need to be addressed immediately. An NPO must always think about their mandate and achieving their objectives, while at the same time ensuring that they are sustainable. The NPO must never lose sight of its mandate - to do good.

A nonprofit may consider focusing on achieving great impact and results with the idea that they will receive further funding down the road. One may even argue that it may even be wise to do so at a cost to their sustainability. In other words, use some of their reserves to achieve impact, hence, incur a deficit to achieve great results which could have the effect of driving more donor revenue. This is a very risky strategy, but at times it may be the best strategy. Due to the risk of this strategy, there should be a cost-benefit done and the results of this strategy should be well documented and reported on.

A less risky strategy would be to find a new project and ensure that results are optimal and well documented. It is important to report on your successes but also on your failures. If a project is not successful, it is best to admit that the project did not meet expectations. It may be due to circumstances beyond your control, but best to own up. When a nonprofit is acting in optimal conditions, they are not required to chase donors, rather donors will be actively seeking to work with you. Part of this process is admitting to your failures and also showcasing your successes. If 25% of your projects are not achieving expected results and 75% are surpassing expected results, this is a good thing. Spend 25% of your reports showing the lack of results and 75% of your time showcasing the positive results, you will earn more trust by being upfront and honest.

The yin and yang must always be in balance, focusing on one at the expense of the other will lead to a poor result. In the case of an NPO, one must focus on delivering impact and maintaining sustainability. In the ideal world, every transaction would be both positive for impact and sustainability, but the reality is not as such. Some transactions will be positive for both impact and profitability, some will benefit impact at the expense of sustainability and others will benefit sustainability at the expense of impact, but only temporarily. In the end, the main goal is to balance both. You cannot have a successful NPO without delivering positive impact and you equally cannot have a successful NPO that runs out of money.

It is also important to point out that companies have a yin and yang as well. A company may set out to deliver the best computers or the best cellphone or deliver the best news, this would be their yin. To achieve their yin, they also must have strong yang. You will not be able to deliver the best computers if you are incurring losses every year. If we look at it from the perspective of the company or NPO, they are both concerned with both yin and yang or impact and sustainability or in the case of companies it could be their mission statement and their profitability, respectively.

For companies, the shareholders are generally, but not always, more concerned with the profitability and less with the mission statement. An investor is generally looking for returns on their investments and increases in share prices, which comes from increases in profits. Hence, the shareholder is primarily concerned with profitability or the yang of a company. On the other hand, while there is generally no counterpart to shareholders, the one that comes the closest would be the donors, their interest is generally not on the sustainability but is rather focused on the impact. Hence, their focus is far greater on the yin.

These key differences between what the focus is for the investors of a company and the contributors to a nonprofit is critical to understanding why these two entities are so different, and why some things may work for one but not the other.

# CHAPTER 4 - BASIC ACCOUNTING PRINCIPLES

In order to understand a nonprofit, you must be able to understand how a business operates and to do that you must understand some degree of accounting principles. Not being able to read financial statements at a comfortable level will make understanding how a business or a nonprofit works all that much more challenging.

The nonprofit has an additional challenge with regards to finance and accounting, these accounting principles are slightly changed to fit the business of nonprofits. First, we must understand the basics of these principles and then how they apply to nonprofits.

A challenge that many nonprofits fall into is that many members of key management have very little understanding of this. One does not have to take a course for months, but an hour or two to understand the concepts is required for any nonprofit executive team to excel.

It is important to understand the basic principles of accounting before we can delve into any differences between for-profit organizations (FPO) and nonprofit organizations.

## Balance Sheet and Income Statement

We will start with the two most important financial statements for any business. This would be the income statement and the balance sheet. Depending on who you ask, when you ask and the particular circumstance of an organization, one financial statement may be more important than the other. When we look at various generally accepted accounting principles (GAAP) across the globe, we can see that certain countries have put more emphasis on the balance sheet and others more importance on the income statement. This is where the philosophy of accounting will come into play, but we will review this later. One thing to note is that historically, if we compare Canadian GAAP with United States GAAP, the Canadian version is prepared more with an income statement philosophy and the US GAAP has used more of a balance sheet philosophy. There are times when a policy may be better for one statement and worse for the other, the philosophy is determined by which statement is felt should be the dominant one where a policy has a trade-off.

Now, as International Financial Reporting Standards (IFRS) are becoming more widely accepted, this approach uses more of an income statement approach. This makes good sense, for the most part, when we evaluate a stock, one key indicator is its earnings or its income, which is derived from the income statement. The balance sheet is more used to ensure that the entity is a going concern and whether it can meet its cash obligations. Hence, one may not want to invest in a company that is covered in debt and has very few assets. Although at the end of the day, if this company is expected to earn millions and grow at a very high rate, this will likely have a much larger effect than the balance sheet, in determining the share prices and the company's overall valuation. The share price multiplied by the outstanding shares is equal to its valuation.

## Income Statement

Starting with the income statement; there are two main parts, there is your revenue section and there are your costs or expenses section. The difference between those two determines your net profit or your net loss when your expenses exceed your revenues. For now, we will ignore taxes, but they also form an important aspect, but more so for the FPO than the NPO.

The standard definition of revenue is fees earned by providing a service or sales earned by selling goods. Hence, for the most part, revenues are derived from selling services or goods, as well, revenue can be earned through investments, such as earning interest income or gains on sales of stocks. We will not cover all the major forms of revenue, but some of the major ones are the following:

**Sales Revenue** - the sale of goods or services

**Interest Revenue**, the earning of interest through an interest-bearing investment.

**Gain on sales**, this could be the gain on any sale which is not generally part of your normal business.

**Donor Revenue**, revenue derived from donor agreements, this is primarily for nonprofits and generally the main source of income for most nonprofits.

The revenue side of your income statement would consist of all the revenue throughout the year. A major distinction between the balance sheet and the income statement is that the income statement covers a period of time, generally a one year period, while the balance sheet is a snapshot and hence, it is reported as at one day or one point in time. When reviewing any audited financial report, you will see the following for Income statements, "For the year ending...date.", while a balance sheet will have the following text, "As at ....date"

Expenses can be defined as the reduction in assets during the year for the receipt of goods or services which are then used or consumed. Hence, if you pay for salaries, the services are used and your assets have been reduced or your liabilities have been increased due to the occurrence of this expense. As an example, if you use a car for one year, that asset will have depreciated in value and that decrease in value is termed depreciation expense or some call it amortization expense. These expenses are used operationally to help drive revenue. The most typical expenses would be; salaries, rent, interest expense, consultant expense, depreciation, cost of goods sold, electricity, fuel, supplies and there are many more. These expenses are used in the daily operation of their business.

## Cash Basis versus Accrual Basis of Accounting

This is a critical concept in accounting and one that qualified accountants understand intrinsically but if you are not a qualified accountant, such as a CPA, CA or CMA, you may not be aware of this distinction. It is common to think that the cash basis is what drives accounting, and while part of that is true, by far the stronger driver is the accrual basis. Expressions like "cash is king", have validity but in accounting accrual is king.

The cash basis of accounting uses the concept of cash to determine an expense, hence if it is paid, then it is an expense. This is true for both revenues and expenses. The reality is that this way of doing accounting does not give the best picture and this is why it is no longer used with most, if not all, GAAP.

The accrual basis of accounting looks to determine expenses and revenues based on either occurrence or earning, in the case of expenses and revenues respectively. If we look at the purchase of a vehicle for $20,000, with the cash basis of accounting the full cost of that vehicle would be expensed in the year of purchase. While with the accrual basis of accounting, that asset still has value, as such, it will be capitalized and then amortized or depreciated over its useful life. If the car has a useful life of ten years and zero residual value, you would expense it at $2,000 per year. This is very different from expensing it all at once and then no charge for the next nine years. At the end of ten years, both systems of accounting would have charged the full $20,000 as expenses.

If we look at an example from the revenue side, we could see that when we look at sales, there may be many vendors that sell with issuing accounts receivable. In accrual accounting, the sales revenue would be recorded when the sale has been earned, normally at the time of sale for goods. While, with the cash basis, this recording of revenue would be recorded at the time of receipt of cash.

Another example to illustrate further is to imagine a bond, that pays double the value in ten years, hence, an imputed rate of over 8%. If the face value of the bond is $1 M and after ten years, the company pays back $2 M. According to the cash basis of accounting, there would be no recognition of interest revenue until the company redeems the bond at $2 M, in that year they would record interest revenue of $1 M. The accrual basis of accounting records interest revenue of $100 K per year over the full ten year period.

With these two examples, it is easy to see that the accrual basis has an effect of smoothing out large revenues or expenses that would be recorded all at once with the cash basis. This is critical, as it improves the stability of earnings and the income statement. This provides a much better ability to value a company than the cash basis approach. It is far easier to see trends with both expenses and revenues under the accrual compared to those under the cash basis.

Let us look at vacation expense, with the cash basis this is expensed when paid. Hence, when a person has a balance of 50 days of vacation pay built up there is no recognition of that expense. However, with the accrual basis of accounting, there would be an accrual made by the year-end to ensure that there is an accrual for that expense. If that person has a daily cost of $1,000, then a $50,000 accrual would need to be made under the accrual basis of accounting. This is because the employee has earned that vacation, hence, the cost has been incurred.

Under the cash basis, if the person did not go on vacation during the year, there would be no charge for that vacation.

### Matching Principle

This follows the matching principle and is key to the accrual basis of accounting. In essence, you match the expenses to the period in which they have been incurred and you match revenues to the period in which they are earned. The end result is a much better presentation of the income statement. If you consider many of these examples, you will see that the cash basis has periods where there is a very large recording of expenses or revenues and then periods where the expenses are nil. This has the effect of greatly destabilizing the income statement and taking away from the predictability of profits. For this and many other reasons, the cash basis of accounting is very rarely used.

In order to understand finance, one needs to understand the balance sheet and the income statement, it is very challenging to understand these statements without a basic understanding of accounting principles. The concept of accrual accounting using the matching principle is one of the fundamental concepts that must be understood for any understanding of accounting, whether it be in the for-profit environment or nonprofit environment.

In a nonprofit environment, for the most part, they follow the accrual basis of accounting, however, many still use the cash basis of accounting when recording expenses for capital assets. Most will expense the full cost of a car in the year of purchase or the full cost of a building in the year of purchase or construction. This is clearly against the matching principle and the accrual basis of accounting. It is widely done because it simplifies the accounting for both the donors and the NPO. This may start to change with the acceptance of IFRS, but we will cover this in later chapters.

### Balance Sheet

The balance sheet is the second most important financial statement of a company and some still consider it to be the most important. The two main philosophies of accounting can be broken down into two main branches, the ones that deem the balance sheet as the more important and the other that considers the income statement more important. The standard US GAAP used to follow a balance sheet philosophy, hence, when a treatment had to be decided on, it would decide on that policy with a slight preference to maintaining a truer reflection of the balance sheet, while other GAAP, such as the UK or Canadian GAAP gave preference to the Income Statement, to present a truer reflection of the income statement. The US is shifting to IFRS which gives more preference to the Income Statement. As a result, this change is more dramatic in the USA and less so in both the UK and Canada.

The balance sheet is comprised of three main areas, the assets, the liabilities, and equity. There is a simple formula for the balance sheet: Assets = Liabilities + Equity or A=L+E

It can easily be remembered by thinking of ALE.

### Assets
When looking at a balance sheet the first item presented is Assets. Assets can be defined as items, whether tangible or intangible, that is owned or controlled by a company, that can be used to provide future positive economic value. Some examples of assets are; Cash, Investments, Buildings, Land, Accounts Receivables, Loans Receivables, Mortgage Receivables, Copyrights, Goodwill and many others.

Assets are generally divided by short term and long term assets. The short assets are assets that can be liquidated very quickly and would include the following: Cash, investments, gold, silver, accounts receivable, the current portion of loans and others. The long term assets would include those assets that are not likely to be used within a year, they would include such items as Land, Buildings, Vehicles, Long Term Loans Receivables, the non-current portion of mortgage receivables, and others.

Once you have put the value of all the current assets, you then add these to get a value for total current assets, then you can prepare the total of all the long term assets. This will then provide two sub-totals. Finally, the sum of these will give you your total Assets. This is the first half of the equation A=L+E

## Liabilities

Liabilities is the second major part of the balance sheet. A liability can be defined as the requirement of a company to use assets in the future as a result of past events. The company has little or no control to avoid these reductions in assets. Some key liabilities would include the following: Accounts Payable, Accrued Vacation Pay, Loans Payable, unearned revenue, bonds payable, Lease Payables, and others.

Similar to assets, Liabilities are divided into current and long term. The basic principle is that current liabilities must be paid within the next fiscal year, while long term will be paid anytime after that. Common current liabilities would include; accounts payable, trade payables, the current portion of lease payables, notes payables and loans payables. While long-term liabilities would include the non-current portion of loan payables, lease payables, bond payables, and others.

There would be a sub-total for both the Current and Long-Term Liabilities and a total for all Liabilities which would include both sub-totals.

## Equity

The final element to a balance sheet is equity and this part finalizes the equation: A = L + E

One can also look at equity as the equation E = A - L, which follows the same logic of the formula above. When we consider the equity we have in a house, we look at the value of the house, less any outstanding loan or mortgage. Hence, if we have a house valued at \$250 K, and a mortgage of \$150 K, we could say that we have $100 K of equity in that property.

Equity has two main components, the first is the capital, this is the sum of funds used by the shareholders to create the company. This could be anywhere from $1 to millions of dollars. It is basically the investment given to the company to start.

The next most important component is Retained Earnings, this is the sum of all profit and losses since inception and less the total amount of dividends paid since inception. This balance generally presents the most significant portion of equity. The size of the retained earnings is often indicative of a well-run company. Some companies will pay a significant amount in dividends and others may not. This should also be taken into account when looking at the health of a company through the balance sheet.

Dividends are not expenses on the income statement, hence, the amount of dividends a company gives plays a lesser role in the value of a stock when you use the income statement for valuation purposes. A company that pays dividends regularly may be attractive to investors that are looking for a cash return prior to selling.

Equity does not have a current or long term division, all of equity by nature is long term.

These form the primary components of your balance sheet. There are some other accounts that are quite common so we will quickly explain their meaning:

### Contra-Asset Account

This account comes up frequently and is within most balance sheets of any company. It is defined as exactly the term applies, it is against an asset account. The most common example of a contra-asset account is accumulated depreciation.

To illustrate how this contra-asset account works, we will look at a building that has a cost of $40 M, let us assume it has a useful life of forty years and no residual value. In this case, you will depreciate the building by $1 M per year.

The accounting entry each year will look as follows:

| Description | Debit | Credit |
|---|---|---|
| Depreciation Expense | $1 M | |
| Accumulated-Depr Building | | $1 M |

The brackets are there to indicate a credit, while positive figures indicate a debit. Notice that the entry was not the following:

| Description | Debit | Credit |
|---|---|---|
| Depreciation Expense | $1 M | |
| Building | | $1 M |

At the end of one year if we look at the asset on the balance sheet showing this building it will look as follows:

| | |
|---|---|
| Building | $40,000,000 |
| Less Accumulated Depreciation | $1,000,000 |
| Balance | $39,000,000 |

Hence, on the balance sheet, you will see both the asset and the contra-asset. Now under IFRS, this approach is different, but we will cover that in a later chapter.

In the case of an NPO, a very important liability to look at is the unearned revenue or Unearned Donor Revenue, this is the balance of receipts from donors less any realized revenue. Hence, a donor may contribute $5 M in December, but if there have not been any costs incurred to date, hence, that grant would yield no earned revenue, as such, the full balance would be shown as a liability as unearned revenue, assuming the grant is a restricted grant. Some unrestricted grants can be fully recognized as revenue, but this would be determined according to the exact terms of the unrestricted grant. Most grants are restricted grants and as such, there should be no recognition of any revenue in this case, and the full amount should show up as a liability. The transaction to record the receipt of funds would be as follows:

| Description | Debit | Credit |
|---|---|---|
| Cash | 5,000,000 | |
| Unearned Donor Revenue | | 5,000,000 |

Cash is an asset account and Unearned Donor Revenue is a liability account. There would be no effect on the income statement and as well, the reserves would remain unaffected by this transaction.

If on the other hand, this was a fully unrestricted fund and the donor intention was to be used for future use and it is allowed to create a surplus, the transaction would look as follows:

| Description | Debit | Credit |
|---|---|---|
| Cash | 5,000,000 | |
| Donor Revenue | | 5,000,000 |

This increases the income statement, as the donor revenue is a revenue line item. This would then lead to an increase in Surplus for the year, which would result in an increase in reserves for the year. Hence, the balance sheet would have an increase in assets (Cash) for $ 5 M, but it would also have an increase in Reserves for $ 5 M, there would be no increase in liability. We will discuss reserves later, but for now it can be seen as very similar to retained earnings, it is basically the summation of all surpluses and deficits since inception of the nonprofit, they do not have the equivalent of dividends in the nonprofit environment.

The difference in accounting for a restricted grand and an unrestricted grant can be quite significant as demonstrated in this example.

There are also times when a restricted grant and an unrestricted grant will end up in very little difference overall. If we take a restricted grant that requires only the use of consultants and has a value of $ 5 M for one year, if this is fully spent in the year, it will result in the following transactions.

**Upon signing**

| Description | Debit | Credit |
|---|---|---|
| Cash | 5,000,000 | |
| Unearned Donor Revenue | | 5,000,000 |

Then after a year of paying consulting fees, they will have the following entry for the payment of consultants during the year.

| Description | Debit | Credit |
|---|---|---|
| Consultant Expenses | 5,000,000 | |
| Cash | | 5,000,000 |

This transaction will trigger the realization of revenue, hence, the following transaction will be needed:

| Description | Debit | Credit |
|---|---|---|
| Unearned Donor Revenue | 5,000,000 | |
| Donor Revenue | | 5,000,000 |

The net results of these transactions will have no effect on assets or liabilities. The income statement will show the following

| Description | Debit | Credit |
|---|---|---|
| Donor Revenue | | 5,000,000 |
| Consultant Expense | 5,000,000 | |

While if the same transactions were to be incurred with an unrestricted grant it, will be as follows:

**For the initial transaction:**

| Description | Debit | Credit |
|---|---|---|
| Cash | 5,000,000 | |
| Donor Revenue | | 5,000,000 |

**Then for the payment of consultants:**

| Description | Debit | Credit |
|---|---|---|
| Consultant Expenses | 5,000,000 | |
| Cash | | 5,000,000 |

The net effect here yields no difference between the two grants.

# CHAPTER 5 - NONPROFIT ACCOUNTING

A nyone that decides to work in a nonprofit and especially those that are at higher levels that would like to influence the success of the nonprofit must understand some accounting principles and how those can be very different in nonprofits. It is not uncommon for some individuals to rise to the rank of Director and above at a nonprofit and still not understand how nonprofit accounting differs from for-profit. It is not to say that they should spend two years studying but it is critical to spend two to three days at some point, to understand the words that you may have to use every day.

**Understanding Nonprofit Accounting**

How much the executive team understands the financial accounting will have a positive effect on its ability to be successful. The reality is that if one is to ask most director-level staff at many nonprofits, a simple question such as why can a restricted grant never result in a surplus. Most would not be able to correctly state the true reason. The real answer is quite simple, a surplus could not be possible because one can only recognize revenue on this grant as one recognizes the expense. Hence, by this definition, the revenues can never exceed the expenses, therefore no surplus can be created by a restricted grant. There are some further complexities, but the basic understanding is required first.

For a Certified Public Accountant or a Chartered Accountant, accounting is very simple and similar to speaking a basic language. You may hear terms like debits and credits, accrual accounting, IFRS, assets, liabilities, equity and retained earnings. To a layperson, this can be quite confusing. Then, when you add in the concept of nonprofit into the mix it can get much more complex rather quickly.

We will focus on the underlying terms that you need to be able to understand the basics of accounting in a general sense within the profit world.

**Balance Sheet versus Statement of Financial Position**
We will start with the balance sheet. The balance sheet follows the standard formula: $A = L + E$, for beer lovers, this can be remembered by memorizing a pint, kidding aside, remember it by the word Ale, as in a Pale Ale.

The A represents Assets, the L represents Liabilities and the E represents Equity. The understanding of this is critical to understanding the balance sheet. As well, a balance sheet is a snapshot in time, think of it as a photograph of the company as at a certain date. When you review the balance sheet of any company it will state the following "As at Date X" hence it may be "As at December 31, 2018", this would be the balance sheet for the year ending 2018. This is opposed to an income statement which is not a snapshot but rather the cumulative total for the year. In the nonprofit environment, many things change, the first is that the nonprofits do not have a Balance Sheet, they have a statement called Statement of Financial Position, it is very similar but different. This statement is also broken down by Assets and Liabilities, but there is no equity in a nonprofit. Instead, in the nonprofit they have net assets. The net assets is similar to Equity, but instead it is the summation of all the years surpluses and deficits. Hence, the formula in the nonprofit becomes A= L+N. Net assets is actually quite easy to calculate, you simply take your assets and subtract your liabilities. Reserves is an important component of net assets. In short, a reserves can come in the form of unrestricted funding or as a surplus. Reserves is a component of net assets. These reserves can be used to purchase long term assets such as a building. When a building is purchased through reserves and capitalized by the nonprofit, the reserves are decreased but the net assets are not decreased. This is one reason why reserves and net assets are not the same, another reason is that a donor may give a contribution as a fund, which is not allowed to be spent but only the revenues can be used. In this case, this grant would be part of net assets but not part of reserves. Reserves are that component of net assets that are not already used for capital assets and are completely flexible in their use, or free of restrictions from a donor. We will cover reserves in more detail in a later chapter, but it is important to get an understanding of the difference from net assets and reserves at this juncture.

**For-Profit Income Statement**
In the for-profit environment, the income statement has three main components, revenues, costs and the difference, which results in profit or loss, this sheet is often called the P&L for profit and loss. The income statement in a set of financial statements is usually stated for the year ending, hence, these statements will have the following terms "For the year ending Date X" or as an example. "For the Year Ending December 31, 2018". This is the sum of activities for the entire year. While in the nonprofit environment there is no concept of profit, hence, nonprofits do not have a P&L or Income Statement, rather they have a Statement of Activities, this follows a similar approach, the first section covers revenues and the expenses is covered in the second section.

**Some key definitions:**

**Assets:**
A tangible or intangible item that is owned or controlled by the company to produce positive economic value in the current or future is an asset.
From IFRS - an asset is a resource controlled by the enterprise as a result of past events and from which future economic benefits are expected to flow to the enterprise.

**Some common examples of Assets are:**

Cash, Accounts Receivable,Land, Building,Loans Receivable and others.

**Liabilities:**
This is the opposite of an asset, it is a future obligation to give up some assets or future benefits that the company must meet.

It can be defined as follows: - Liabilities are a result of past transactions that require the future sacrifice of economic bene-fit, which is outside of the control of the entity.

Liabilities can also be broken down into Current and Long Term.

**Some examples of liabilities are the following**:

Accounts Payable, Loans Payable,Mortgage Payable,Bank Debt and others.

On the balance sheet, you break these down into current and long term, the current is what is due to be paid within the next fiscal year and long term is anything that is payable beyond one fiscal year. Hence, if I have a bank loan of $100 K and $10 K of that is payable in the next fiscal year, the liability would be broken down as follows:

**Liabilities**

**Current**
Bank Loan          10,000

### Long Term
Bank Loan        90,000

You can see that the total is still $100 K, but it is broken between the current portion and the long term portion.

The same logic is applied to Assets, you have the current portion and the non-current portion. Some assets like Cash, have no due date and hence are all current. But a loan receivable could have a current portion and a non-current portion or a long term portion.

On the other hand Assets such as Land, do not have a current portion, unless there is a plan to sell that land within the year, otherwise, by default, it falls into the long term side and not the current side.

You follow this logic for each asset and each liability and that is how you create the majority of your balance sheet. The last item on your balance sheet is your E or your Equity. The equity of a company is formed by two main items, the first is the Capital of the company, this is the sum that was originally given to the company to begin operations. Assume a company is brand new and has no operations and on the first day, the owners contribute a piece of land worth $100 K to that company. The assets would have a value of $100 K, there would be no liability but there would be Capital of $100 K. Each time the owners contribute to the company this effects its equity.

The other major item that forms part of equity is Retained Earnings, this is the sum of all earnings of the prior years since inception. Hence, if a company has been earning $25 K per year and has existed for 10 years, it will have retained earnings of $250 K, assuming no dividends were paid out.

After ten years the Equity portion of this company could look as follows:

### Equity

Capital        100,000

Retained Earnings          250,000

**Total Equity          350,000**

The Assets, Liabilities, and Equity are the three components to any balance sheet. We will get to how these differ in a nonprofit environment after we review the income statement.

### Income Statement/Profit & Loss versus Statement of Activities

The income statement is also very simply broken down into three main sections, they are Revenue, Expenses, and Profit or Loss. The formula is quite simple and it is as follows: P = R - E (Profits = Revenue less Expenses).

Stated out it is the profit is equal to the revenue less the expenses if expenses are greater than the revenue then it is no longer a profit but a loss or a deficit. One always prefers that your revenues are greater than your expenses, except when it comes to paying taxes. Humor aside, it is always better to have a tax liability this implies that your company is profitable and a profitable company that owes taxes is far better than a losing company that does not owe taxes.

### Revenue

The definition of revenue is the income that is brought in by a company through its sale of goods or services. As mentioned earlier, in the income statement the revenues are stated during a set period of time, normally the year ending. Hence, they are normally for the year ending on a given date. There are exceptions to this, but for now, we will not go into those exceptions.

In the nonprofit environment, rather than a P&L or Income Statement, they have a statement called Statement of Activities, which is very analogous, but instead or profit or loss, they have surplus or deficit.

### Expense

The definition of expense is the use of assets in a normal course of business to deliver services or produce goods for sale. Hence, this is the costs that are incurred to produce or deliver the goods and services that produced the revenues.

## Accrual Basis of Accounting versus Cash Basis

At this point, it is critical to review the two types of accounting:
1. Accrual Accounting
2. Cash Basis

Accrual accounting is the modern generally accepted form of accounting throughout the world. This follows the matching principle. Hence, you only realize revenues when they are earned and only realize expenses when they are incurred.

The cash basis is an outdated model and it would follow the logic of recording items when the cash is paid or received. This can lead to a very different results than through accrual accounting. The concept of cash is still very important and there is another financial statement that explains the changes in cash position during the year. If a company is profitable but is struggling with cash flow, this could have a serious negative effect if that cash flow issue is not resolved.

Practically speaking, what does accrual accounting mean. One major difference would be the use of Accounts Receivable, these are for sales but are not immediately sold for cash. On the cash basis approach, one would not recognize that sale until cash is received, but with accrual accounting, one would recognize that sale, prior to receiving cash.

In expense terms, this issue is even more critical. A main component of salaries could be the built-up vacation leave, with cash accounting, you only record this expense when paid, but with accrual accounting, you expense this as it is earned by the employees.

Now, you have the ability to prepare an income statement, also known as a profit and loss statement or 'P & L' for short.

## Nonprofit Accounting

So how does nonprofit accounting differ from profit accounting? The profit world, primarily, focuses on accrual accounting, while the nonprofit world, for the most part, has used a hybrid approach to accounting. This is starting to change with nonprofits being forced to use Internationally Accepted Finance Reporting Standards (IFRS), the problem is that even IFRS has stated that it has not completely developed the rules for nonprofits. This makes sense because there are some difficulties in doing such a switch, with a system that has always been hybrid, I.e. the accounting in nonprofits. In the chapter on IFRS, we will dive into this deeper.

The first area to understand in the nonprofit world is the concept of nonprofit. This is an important distinction and one that must be understood to understand the whole concept of nonprofits. nonprofits generally get their funding through grants and usually, these grants are termed restricted grants or they are restrictive in nature. There are also some that are unrestricted that we will discuss shortly. With a restricted grant, there is no way to have a surplus or a deficit (within the accounting of that grant). The mechanics of this are simple when one recognizes an expense for a given grant one can also recognize the revenue, but no more and no less. Hence, through this mechanism, the expenses will always equal the revenues and therefore, there will never be a profit or a loss. A grant could also never have a loss, an expense cannot be recorded if it is not a valid expense, and as such, only valid expenses will lead to revenue recognition. If the grant were to start overspending, technically these would not be valid expenses. Hence, they would need to be charged to another grant or to the NPO itself.

In nonprofits, the revenue side has another important step to be recognized, you cannot recognize any revenue before an expense is incurred and recognized. If the expenses are for items such as salaries, then one can say that this is following the accrual basis.

If we take a situation where a donor gives a grant that is given to the grantee for the purposes of purchasing a building or building one. Let us say the amount is $5 M. Prior to IFRS, the method was purely cash basis for assets, that is the building would be charged as an expense and the revenue would all be realized as income (assuming the building was purchased and/or built within the year). This goes against accrual accounting, as the building still has value and still is an asset, hence, it should not be fully expensed in one year, but rather it should be capitalized and expensed throughout its useful life.

Let us examine the situation of the purchase of a building on the last day of the year and compare the treatment from a non-profit and profit perspective.

**Profit Method**

| Description | Debit | Credit |
|---|---|---|
| Building | 5,000,000 | |
| Cash | | 5,000,000 |

Let us assume that the owners first gave $5 M in capital to buy the building

| Description | Debit | Credit |
|---|---|---|
| Cash | 5,000,000 | |
| Capital | | 5,000,000 |

In the end, assuming this was the only transaction it will look as follows:

Balance Sheet

| | |
|---|---|
| Building | 5,000,000 |
| Cash | 0 |

| | |
|---|---|
| Liabilities | 0 |
| Equity | |
| Capital | 5,000,000 |

There would be no income statement, as there were no expenses or revenues during the year

**Nonprofit Method**

Donor gives $5 M:

| Description | Debit | Credit |
|---|---|---|
| Cash | 5,000,000 | |
| Donor Liability | | 5,000,000 |

Then buys the building

| Description | Debit | Credit |
|---|---|---|
| Building | 5,000,000 | |
| Cash | | 5,000,000 |

Now some additional transactions that are necessary in the nonprofit world

| Description | Debit | Credit |
|---|---|---|
| Revenues | 5,000,000 | |
| Building Expense | | 5,000,000 |

| Description | Debit | Credit |
|---|---|---|
| Donor Liability | 5,000,000 | |
| Building | | 5,000,000 |

The sum of this leaves a balance sheet of no assets, no liabilities and no equity, while the income statement is as follows

**Revenues**

Donor revenue          5,000,000

**Expenses**

Building Expense       5,000,000

**Profit**                      0

One can see that the way an asset is treated in nonprofit accounting is completely different and breaks many rules with regards to the accrual basis of accounting. This is starting to change with the adoption of IFRS.

Now if we are to adopt an accrual stance to this transaction, it is about to get far more complex to be able to handle it properly. The first critical item is that in accrual accounting there should be no expense on that asset (the building) the reason for this is that it was bought on the last day of the year and hence there is no depreciation expense yet. In the next year, there will be an expense and that would be equal to the difference from cost and residual value divided by useful life. Hence, if the purchase price is $5 M and let's assume it has a useful life of 40 years and a residual value of $1 M, then accrual accounting would expect a $100 K depreciation or amortization expense per year. This would be charged as the following:

| Description | Debit | Credit |
|---|---|---|
| Depreciation expense | 100,000 | |
| Accumulated Depreciation | | 100,000 |

Accumulated Depreciation is a contra-asset account. Hence, it reduces the value of the asset.

In the nonprofit environment, assuming that one followed

the accrual basis of recording assets, the treatment would be slightly more complex. It would be as follows:

| Description | Debit | Credit |
|---|---|---|
| Depreciation Expense | 100,000 | |
| Accumulated Depreciation | | 100,000 |
| Revenues | | 100,000 |
| Donor Liability | 100,000 | |

In this case, the depreciation expense would cause the realization of revenue from the donor and this would result in an increase in the accumulated depreciation and the reduction of the donor liability. Since there is no revenue recognition on the asset, the contribution cannot go to equity, hence, it must go to liabilities, as a donor liability. It would also mean that in the first year, there could be no revenue or expense recognized. In the first year, using this method there would be no income statement and there would be a balance sheet with an asset of the building and a liability to the donor each for $5 M. This would then be expensed over the next 40 years. The issue with this is that the liability would remain on the books for forty years. The advantage of this is that it does follow a proper accrual process. The other challenge is that the donor would not like to have to receive reports for the next forty years to see their grant paid off. This can also be achieved by having reports that are sent to the donors that are prepared by the accepted practices by both donor and the nonprofit organization (NPO). Hence, a report could be given to the donor that shows the full utilization of the grant in one year and explains how the grant will be accounted for in accounting terms. This may seem unusual to many, however, this is already common practice with any profit organization. Every profit organization also prepares a tax return, the tax rules are sometimes quite different from IFRS and GAAP and hence are prepared under different policies.

Your taxable income is not always equal to your Net Income Before Tax, this is due to permanent and timing differences within the tax code. These differences can give rise to Deferred Income Taxes, we will explain this concept in another publication.

Hence, the way to resolve this one for all parties is to have the NPO follow the accrual process all the way through but set up Deferred Revenue Account, which is a liability and then recognize the revenue over the years and offset the Deferred Revenue Account. Then there would need to be a separate report that goes to the donor that shows the use of the donor funds. This report would be prepared along the traditional rules but would also explicitly state the accounting treatment that would follow. So the donors can understand what is happening to their funds and how their contribution affects the income statement and balance sheet. A donor may get confused to see a $5 M expense on their report and then see an audited statement showing no expense. This would be covered in the notes to the financial statement and the report that is given to the donor.

By doing this, the nonprofit can follow the rules of the accrual basis of accounting and ensure their donor reporting is not altered too greatly. This would also present a significant improvement in the overall reporting both on their income statement and their balance sheet, both would present a truer reflection of reality. As well, the auditors would no longer need to issue a qualification in their opinion. One may feel that this is overly complex, but the reality is most reporting systems can prepare this automatically without much intervention from the user.

## Statement of Functional Expense

With regards to financial statements for nonprofits, the nonprofits have a statement called Statement of Functional Expenses, there is no equivalent to this in the for-profit environment, as this is important to nonprofits but not to for-profit. It is important to always keep in mind that the rationales for these two different types of entities are very different. When looking at this statement, the distinction between project costs and non-project costs become very crucial. When contributing to a nonprofit, an individual or donor would like to see that a high level of contributions goes towards projects and less to non-project costs or administration.

## Statement of Shareholders' Equity

This is a statement that only exists in the for-profit environment, as there is no equity in the nonprofit environment. There are times when some nonprofits issue a statement called, Statement of Changes in Net Assets, which is quite similar.

An understanding of these key principles of accounting in nonprofits is critical to understanding how a nonprofit works. The nonprofit still functions as a business, but just not a business that aims for profits.

# CHAPTER 6 - FULL COST ACCOUNTING IN NONPROFITS

The term full cost accounting when applied to nonprofits or NPO's generally is the ability to charge the full cost for a project. What does this really mean? With any project, there will be overhead costs that may be indirectly or directly related to a given project. A project with donor X may allow for certain staff costs, some direct costs, such as training or materials, some expenses such as rent and then perhaps a 15% admin cost or overhead cost.

The idea here is that you should charge the full cost, not more and not less. If to do a given project Y, the real costs in total would be $2 M over two years, you do not want to charge $1.5 M and you also do not want to charge $2.5 M for this project. If you are undercharging for a grant, this is fine if you can supplement it with your own funds or if you have a generous pool of unrestricted funds. In essence, you could charge $1.5 M for the project, given that you have other sources of unrestricted funds that can compensate for this or you feel it is worthwhile to use your reserves to cover this. This should be a very rare case and the goal would be to aim to charge the full cost, for all projects.

### Direct and Indirect Costs

If the project has direct costs of $2.0 M and indirect costs of $0.3 M, then you should charge the total of $2.3 M for this project. It would have a budget of $2.0 M and an admin fee of $0.3 M or 15%. The $2 M budget would entail detailed line items such as salaries, rent, materials, training, etc, while the admin would not have details, this would form a pool of expenses and the revenues from the admin side would go against this.

To illustrate the above, let us assume that there is NPO X, that has one grant from one donor for $2 M and includes a $0.3 M amount for admin costs. The NPO has actual overhead costs of $ 300 K and no other costs. During the year the NPO expenses the full amount of $2 M on the project and the full $300 K for overhead costs. The accounting treatment of this would be as follows:

Let's assume the direct costs are $1.5 M of salaries and $0.5 M of goods. During the year, this exact sum is spent, hence the journal entry would be as follows:

| Description | Debit | Credit |
|---|---|---|
| Salary Expense | 1,500,000 | |
| Cash | | 1,500,000 |
| Goods expense | 500,000 | |
| Cash | | 500,000 |

This would be the first transaction, it is important to note that with NPO, there must be an equal and opposite transaction to realize the revenue side. Hence, this transaction is required

| Description | Debit | Credit |
|---|---|---|
| Unearned donor revenue | 2,000,000 | |
| Revenue | | 2,000,000 |

Note: Revenues are generally recorded as credits and hence the negative sign denotes a credit, while positive figures would be debits.

This transaction records the revenue and reduces the donor liability. The first transaction when the NPO received the funds of $2.3 M was as follows:

| Description | Debit | Credit |
|---|---|---|
| Cash | 2,300,000 | |
| Unearned donor revenue | | 2,300,000 |

Along with the initial transaction there is a required transaction to record the 15% admin cost. This one is slightly trickier, it should be recorded as follows, this will move the admin revenues from the donor account to the main account, as a negative expense.

| Description | Debit | Credit |
|---|---|---|
| Admin Expense (Donor) | 300,000 | |
| Admin Expense (Main) | | 300,000 |

This transaction sets up the expense on the donor account and moves a negative expense (revenue) into the main account. It must be set as a negative expense and not as revenue, otherwise, both the revenue and expenses will be overstated.

When realizing the admin expense, one should also move the cash into the proper account, this can be achieved by the following entry which mirrors the above entry:

| Description | Debit | Credit |
|---|---|---|
| Cash (Main acct) | 300,000 | |
| Cash (Donor Acct) | | 300,000 |

Once the admin expenses are paid from the main account, the transaction would look as follows:

| Description | Debit | Credit |
|---|---|---|
| Admin Expense (Main acct) | 300,000 | |
| Cash (Main acct) | | 300,000 |

And finally since, you have recorded an expense on the donor account you must also record the revenue hence, the last transaction for this would be as follows:

| Description | Debit | Credit |
|---|---|---|
| Unearned donor revenue | 300,000 | |
| Donor Revenues | | 300,000 |

The result of these transactions would be the balance sheet would have no assets, no liabilities and no equity. The income statement would show the following:

| Revenues | 2,300,000 |
|---|---|
| **Expenses** | |
| Salaries | 1,500,000 |
| Goods | 500,000 |
| Admin | 300,000 |
| Total | 2,300,000 |
| **Net Profit** | **0** |

One can see that there are a lot more transactions involved in a nonprofit organization compared with a profit organization. Each donor fund should have its own set of accounts or separate trust funds to maintain balances, as such, each transaction will also have a trust fund number and also a project number, at a minimum. The related transactions can be set up automatically by your system for each transaction or it can be done at the end of each month to run automatically. In order to reduce the vast number of transactions, it may be wise to set this every month or every week rather than for each transaction. A daily summary also works very well. To get an idea of the complexity, each transaction that can be charged to a restricted grant, will require a percentage move from the admin fee and as well, the corresponding revenue realization transactions.

There are some major challenges with full cost accounting, the first is estimating the amount of donor grants that one would have for the full year and the actual spend rate. You may have $100 M of donor revenue available to spend in 2019, but if you only spend $80 M, then you will only get 15% of the $80

M or $12 M and not the full $15 M available. This is not such an issue if the spend is caught up during the next year. If you have a situation where your total admin costs are $15 M and you are expecting to have $100 M in funding, but you only get $80 M in funding, even if you spend at 100% of your budget, you will only receive $12 M in funding, but your overheads are $15 M, hence, you will create a deficit of $3 M in the year. As your admin rates are fixed within your budgets, there is little that can be done to correct this situation. The only real option would be to find more donor funding, reduce your admin costs, or get further unrestricted funds to cover this deficit. If the deficit is caused by underspending in one year, then this can be corrected by overspending in the subsequent year or years. One should understand if the cause of any deficit is primarily due to decreased funding or due to a lower spending rate. One is indicative of a serious problem and the other is indicative of a problem that is more easily resolved by increasing the grants spending rates.

## Some Exceptions

There is at least one donor that does allow the NPO to adjust their overhead rate for such events, as such, should there be a loss, the donor would cover this, but as well, should there be a gain, the donor would retain this gain. This is a positive approach, as it gives some of the risks to the donor. One donor is USAID, but only with NPOs that qualify for this treatment. In essence, their overhead rate is flexible with actual results.

## Pros and Cons

There are pros and cons to each approach. In the end, the donors should give grants that are fair and that allow the nonprofits to be self-sustaining. If donors give funding but it is too minimal on admin costs that it forces the NPO to reduce their reserves or use up some other unrestricted grants, then this situation would not be sustainable for the long run. Hence, it is in the best interest of both the NPO and the donor to find an optimal middle ground.

### Defining an Admin Cost

The issue of what is defined as an admin cost plays a major role in this and unfortunately, there can be a lot of different ways to define admin costs and many are valid but there are also ways that these definitions can be adjusted to drive down your overhead or admin rate. In short, the flexibility of these definitions can provide too much leeway for the NPO. For example, if an NPO has an admin rate of 23%, this may be seen as too high by some donors. There is a way to just redefine what is an admin cost and what is a direct project cost, that can have a direct and immediate effect on this. It is not unusual to see an admin rate drop from 25% one year and drop to 15% in the next year, there are occasions where this was done naturally by cutting staff on the admin side or by ramping up operations drastically. However, many times this is due to a redefinition of what is an admin cost and what is not. One may define a staff that is directly funded by a donor as a direct cost, hence, if a finance person or accountant is funded by the donor, then this cost would be project cost and not an admin cost. The problem here is that it would give an advantage to those NPO's that have grants that fund accountants compared with those that do not. Logically, it should be clear that the source of funding should not be the determining factor in whether a cost is an admin or a project cost. What about the case of unrestricted funds, in many cases, a large portion of these funds will go to admin costs or otherwise unfunded costs. If these grants fund admin costs, should they no longer be admin costs? The answer is clearly no, but this is not always how it works in practice.

This is why the admin costs or admin ratio that an NPO gives out should be taken with a grain of salt. There is competition among many NPO's to have lower admin rates and this may cause an institution to take a more radical approach as to how admin costs are defined and hence how they are calculated. If an NPO has a 35% admin rate and they are competing for donor funds where the average is 15%, they will have a difficult time attracting funds. They will be viewed as bloated and less efficient.

The interesting issue is that many nonprofits with a lower rate might actually be less efficient and more bloated but have chosen their definition of admin costs much more advantageously. As a donor who would be choosing which entity to invest with it may be misleading to solely focus on admin rates or to give such a high value on this ratio. One of the most important factors should be the success rate of an entity or perhaps the delivery rate compared to costs.

### Donors are Looking for Impact

The reason a nonprofit is working and the reason a donor funds a given NPO is for their impact. When a donor gives funding to a charity, they are expecting some good to be delivered to the world. So if a donor gives money to fight AIDS, they are expecting either medicine to be delivered in areas that are poor or expecting there to be an information campaign to be delivered to given populations which would then result in a drop in the incidence of AIDS. These deliverables are expected to achieve some outcomes and impact. This is the main reason why a donor would fund an NPO. Hence, it would make sense that a major factor in choosing which NPO to pick would be the success rate of the NPO.

Hence, success rate and delivery rate would be better factors in determining the best suitable NPO, an NPO with a very high admin rate would likely not have a great success rate, for example, if the actual admin costs were 75%, then this NPO would only be delivering 25 cents out of every dollar to projects, this would mean that they are very much bloated and would desperately need to make certain corrections to improve their efficiency by reducing admin costs.

## How do you make a highly efficient NPO?

The first step is to figure out what is your goal? What problem in the world do you want to help improve or solve? Is it poverty? Is it hunger? Is it AIDS? Malaria? You need to have a cause and you need to have some historical results in addressing this cause. The next step is figuring out your ideal mix of admin costs versus non-admin costs, a good range to start at is 15%. Hence, if you have $100 M of total costs, your admin rate should be $15 M, so as a percentage of total costs this is $ 15 M divided by $100 M or 15%, but as a percentage of project costs, it is $15 M divided by $85 M ($100 M - $15 M) or 17.65%. The admin rate is usually calculated as a total admin cost divided by total costs, which include both project costs and admin costs. Understanding this difference can save some nonprofits millions of dollars.

Let us assume for now that you can get about $100 M in funding every year, therefore your ideal admin costs should be about $15 M. Then you must allocate these admin costs to the most efficient admin team that you can figure out. How much is needed for finance, HR, grants unit, fundraising, management, logistics and overheads associated with this? How much of these costs are fixed and how many are variable? This way you can get an idea of your ideal situation.

The same process can be used and should be used for an ongoing NPO. One can look at the breakdown of their costs and their balance sheet and see where they stand and look for the ideal position and where they are on target but more importantly where they are off-target. If the admin cost ratio is getting too high, is this a function of having fewer grants without a corresponding decrease in admin costs or is it due to rising admin costs? Is the lowering of grant revenue permanent or just a temporary dip? This is not always easy to tell, but if the dip has continued for more than two years, it should be viewed as permanent, hence, there should be real changes made to their actual admin costs to correct this. This is for NPO's that are not in ideal conditions if an NPO has endless reserves or has endless unrestricted funds, then they have more leeway to make the changes later. However, it is always best to prepare early. Being financially prudent is great for the nonprofit and also great for the donors who provide funding. Taking this approach even when not necessary will show your donors that you are being financially responsible with their funding and it should also have a positive impact on your delivery and results of the NPO overall.

### Choice of Projects - Donor or Nonprofit

There is also sometimes a divide in where the donor would like to place their funding and projects that the nonprofit would prefer to undertake. The NPO's that are self-sufficient or have a significant amount of unrestricted funding would have the advantage of doing more of what they prefer, while those organizations that are just getting by must go fully in the direction that the donor would like. This is a critical point, as an NPO one must understand that to maintain financial sustainability, one must not overextend themselves or take on too much risk. If a project is not funded and there does not exist sufficient unrestricted funding or reserves, it should not be undertaken, at the very least the cost should be severely minimized. If the project is strategically needed and funding does not exist, one alternative would be to create a minimal team to head up the project until donor funding can help grow the project.

To minimize risk, one must look at their costs that are funded versus their unfunded costs. The first step to doing this would be to put aside your unrestricted funds for now and allocate your restricted grants to your actual costs. Ideally, there should be a strong correlation between your actual costs and your funding. Hence, if your restricted funding amounts to $75 M per year (before admin costs), ideally there would also be a corresponding $75 M of actual costs or estimated actual costs that match to this funding Particularly this is important for staff salaries. If there are $50 M of staff salaries funded within this $75 M funding, these staff must be known, they exist and they are working directly for the projects that are paying for their salary. You do not want to have grants that show $50 M for staff salaries and you have a total of $70 M for staff salaries, this would mean that you now have $20 M of unfunded staff costs. This will quickly eat up whatever unrestricted funding you have.

## Ideal Situation

In an ideal situation where you have funding for your existing costs. What you do not want to have is a mismatch. You could have a situation where you have funding but do not have the matching costs. As an example, if your budget allows for the cost of two medical doctors, but instead you have two Information Technology staff on board. You cannot charge those staff to that project, hence those staff would be unfunded and your funding would not match your costs, this will require you to go out and hire the staff that you have funding for. Ideally, you want the situation to have all of your costs covered and then have some unrestricted funds in reserve. This can help out with funding a given project which is considered necessary but remains unfunded. In the ideal situation, all of your costs are funded by restricted projects and your admin costs are funded by the admin portion of your restricted projects. Then you would have your unrestricted grants as a buffer or in reserve to cover for a rainy day or to take on special projects. Perhaps there is a capital project that you are looking to invest in. Another great use of unrestricted grants is building up your reserves to later use for large capital projects.

The closer that you can get to this situation the closer you will be to true financial stability. If the unrestricted grants are truly unrestricted, these can be brought into revenue during the year and qualify as a surplus then flow into reserves. Reserves would be the result of a surplus and are similar to retained earnings. This would allow you to save to take on capital projects or make some investments with a return, it also gives you the flexibility to take on projects without the corresponding donor funding. This would be critical to starting a new set of projects that may be necessary for the nonprofit but may not be high priority for donors.

### Earned Income comes with Advantages

One of the advantages of an entity that has a large amount of earned income through investments is that gives them a lot of flexibility in choosing their projects and less time is required looking for donor funding. This also allows the NPO to have a very stable level of funding and ensure that the NPO has stable costs and staffing levels. This would have the effect of making the NPO that much more efficient, in the long run.

One good example of this is the International Finance Corporation (IFC) or most any development bank, such as African Development Bank or Asian Development Bank. They often have two main operations, the first is the investment operations and the second is the technical assistance, the full amount of the investment division is funded by earned revenue and a significant part of the technical assistance operations is funded by their earned revenue. The technical assistance side is also funded by donor revenues, but the fact that the critical costs are funded by earned income, this allows them to focus on funding good projects without much risk. It will take decades for many nonprofits to reach this level of earned income, but each nonprofit should strive to achieve a 5% level of earned income as compared to total costs. This small step will give a great boost to the efficiency and financial health of a nonprofit.

**Development Bank Model**
The way that IFC and other development banks, like Asian Development Bank or African Development Bank, work is a great model for others to follow. At times, some may feel that making large surpluses can be seen as a negative, but this view is incorrect. It is by creating this surplus that these nonprofits can do more good in future years and can ensure a stable future in order to help reduce poverty in the world. These earnings allow them to have a going concern and fund their operations without the need to always be at the risk of not attaining funding goals. On the technical assistance side, they do have partnerships with donors and this allows them to have further reach on that side of the operations. One may argue that this is not correct, but if an entity can earn funds while at the same time assisting others and thereby ensure that they can assist more in the future, this is a great model. If these development banks did not have a large amount of earned income, a lot of their efforts would need to be spent every year on fundraising to get the funding required to have this positive effect. This would hamper their results and lead to a lot of uncertainty in funding levels. One must balance impact and sustainability, we will cover this issue in a later chapter. Earned income definitely makes the nonprofit that much more efficient by being able to focus energy on results and not on fundraising, it also has the benefit of giving the nonprofit a greater choice in the direction of their projects. Development banks are able to deliver high impact results due to their financial strength and their ability to generate a steady flow of earned income. This gives them a strong advantage when considering the success of a nonprofit. Being in the position of not having to seek funding has many advantages, other organizations like the Gates Foundation, would also fall into this category.

# CHAPTER 7 -
# FINANCE TEAMS

F or an equal-sized organization in terms of spend and in terms of staffing, one will see marked differences between finance teams for nonprofit and their counterparts in the profit world. The first and most striking difference is the size of the team. The team will generally be much larger in the nonprofit environment, but a lot of this will depend on how the organization is funded. For the most part, nonprofits are funded by restricted grants. This requires a lot more careful examination and preparing annual reports than an unrestricted grant. The average size of these grants plays a vital role. It is roughly the same amount of work to manage a $100 K grant than it is to manage a $10 M grant. Hence, if you have a lot of small grants, you will need to have more finance staff for an equally sized organization.

Imagine two organizations A and B, both have $100 M of annual funding, but in one the average size grant is $10 M and the other organization the average size is $100 K, A will have ten grants to manage and report on while B will have 1,000 grants to report on, requiring far more work and staff hours, hence, more staff.

**Restricted versus Unrestricted Grants**
Another very large factor is whether the grants are restricted

or unrestricted. In simple terms, a restricted grant can only be spent on very specific items and must follow a budget that is approved by the donor and the organization. With unrestricted grants, the funds are given to the organization and there are generally no budgets attached, these funds can be spent in any way the organization feels best. These grants are ideal, from the view or the organization but not always the best from the donors' perspective. It is for this reason that these grants are far less common than restricted grants.

In some cases, the funding is given primarily by one government and the organization tends to be a kind of hybrid government organization. The advantage in this situation is that they will be able to get a large portion of their funding that will be generally quite unrestricted and they will also have guaranteed funding for many years. This allows the entity to search for other funding and potentially also use the government's funding as a kind of subsidy for some of the costs or to help purchase some of the infrastructure, which may be harder to find funding.

At many developmental bank organizations, such as Asian Development Bank, World Bank, International Finance Corporation and many more, a significant part of the funding comes from the entity itself via their earned income. These organizations are in a privileged position as it has significant earned income and could use some of these earnings to fund most of the operations, these costs are funded from the profits or surpluses from the investment part of the operations. This is a critical principle for the successful nonprofit, focusing on strong financial health or sustainability.

**Financially Sustainable**
Another very important factor is whether the operations are at a self-sustaining stage or not there yet. If an entity is losing funding revenues then further efforts must be spent on fundraising, this means spending on grant creation but also budget creation, this will put additional demands on the finance team and other teams within the organization.

Hence, the major contributors that affect the relative size of a finance team within an NPO are:

1. The size of the organization
2. The average size of their grants
3. The nature of the grants, restricted versus unrestricted
4. Whether a large pool of funding exists from a government entity or self-funded (high degree of earned income)
5. Whether the organization is financially stable or going through an economic crisis

All of these factors will play a role in determining the average size of the finance team and relative size as well. Hence, if two equally sized organizations let's call them A and B, but one has a very small average size of their grants, the vast majority are restricted, without a related donor (government or self-funded), and also is in dire straits financially, this will require a much larger team than an organization that has the opposite. The differences may be staggering. This makes comparing apples to apples a lot more challenging. To put this in perspective, it would be like comparing two cars, each of equal capability roughly, let's say we compare a Honda Civic, with a Toyota Corolla, both solid cars. But let us test out the Civic's performance on a good highway and let us test the Corolla in a swamp somewhere. The Civic will run smoothly and get a great mileage per gallon. It will not have issues. The Corolla, on the other hand, will have problems just to move five feet. Hence, if the terrain is very poor you need a stronger, bigger and more expensive car to get moving. In one situation you may be preparing ten reports a month and in the other, you may be preparing 500 a month. In a good situation, you may only need to prepare a few budget proposals a year, but in the other, you may have to prepare a couple of hundred a year.

**Comparing Apples**
This is where the idea of comparing apples to apples has some

issues. One needs to consider the environment that they occupy. In the ideal case, for a nonprofit, they would be able to manage with a very similar size to a profit organization. This could be roughly 1.5%, hence, for an organization of 1,000 staff, a profit organization can have as few as 15 finance staff, perhaps up to 20. This would be very similar to a nonprofit that works in ideal situations, not many grants and a significant supply of unrestricted funds and a financially sustainable situation. If they have a large percentage of restricted funds, this is where it changes drastically, this fact alone could change the average size to 3%. If they have a large number of smaller grants, this change can have a large effect on the size, it could double the size, hence, it could go up to 4 - 6%. In addition to this, if the organization is not financially strong or sustainable, this could increase the size by an additional 1%, at a minimum. Hence an NPO in the worst situation may need a finance team of 7% or more, hence for a staff size of 1,000, the finance team size would need to be 70 staff or more. There is a large distinction between 15 and 70 staff or 1.5% and 7%. One clear thing is that the 7% should not be for the long run, it should be until corrections can be made, to ensure the organization is financially stable again. Steps should be undertaken to increase the average size of the grant, this will have a positive effect on the finance team size. Of course, before this can be done, one should ensure that the NPO is financially stable. You do not want to cut some projects during a time where you are not financially sound. There should also be a focus on getting grants that are unrestricted or partially unrestricted. This will require management to work with donors to find ways that can alleviate this situation by agreeing to some grants that would be unrestricted.

## Expanding Operations

Another reason for an increased finance team size is that an organization may be looking to expand and gain more donor funding, this would require a temporary increase in the finance team and an increase on the fund-raising team side, as well. This would not be permanent but would be until the funding levels have met the target levels. This could occur in a year where the organization decides to focus on growth.

## Percentage of funding in Unrestricted Grants

If we consider the ratio of funds that are unrestricted versus restricted, we can have it fall under these main categories

1. >50% Ideal No real negative effect on finance team staff size
2. 25% to 50% Next to ideal, minimal effect on staff size
3. 15% to 25% Poor situation, this is manageable but will require an increase of 1 to 2%
4. < 15% Very challenging, this will require a significant increase in finance staff to manage

Another factor is the average size of grants and the number of grants as a ratio to staff.

They can be broken as follows:

Percentage of the number of restricted grants to the total number of total staff

1. < 3% Ideal This is 30 grants per thousand staff - no effect
2. 3% - 6% Almost ideal, up to 60 grants per thousand staff
3. 6% - 15% Not good This would be up to 150 grants per thousand staff
4. Over 15% Poor situation This is more than 150 grants per thousand staff

On the whole, a good finance member can manage about 3 - 5 grants, now if you have 5% grants per staff, this would mean that you need one more staff member for each additional 4 grants. Hence, if you have 200 additional grants, you would need an additional 40 staff members or 4% more. This factor depends on the difficulty in reporting, hence, we are taking average cases. Some donor reports are very simple and some are more complex. This factor alone can show how a finance team size is negatively affected by the ratio of grants to staff. Ideally you would like to stay at or below the 3% level, one could go up to the 6% level but above that level, this will cause a significant effect on the finance team staff size and it will become quite difficult to manage. This factor is directly related to the average size of grants, as well.

A financially stable NPO will have a great advantage compared with one that is not stable. The latter will be forced to look for further funding and require going to more donors to make requests. It will also have to manage any deficits occurring and find areas to fix this. This will have a significant effect on the finance team. It could be that this issue alone could increase the staff size by 1%, hence those that face these issues will need to have an extra 1% staff to cover this. An NPO in a poor financial state will be less likely to turn down small grants, as such, they will tend to have a higher number of grants per thousand staff, this will also have a negative effect on the overall demands on the finance team.

**Ideal Team Size**

Hence, to determine the proper or appropriate size of a finance team for a given NPO, one would need to look at all of the above factors mentioned. Then one could estimate the number of staff that the finance team should have. When looking over this, one can see in an ideal situation the finance team staff size should be about 1.5% - 2%, while in very poor conditions the finance team size could be anywhere from 5% - 7%. Looking at the relative finance team size will tell you nothing about the efficiency without taking into account these factors.

It is critical to compare finance teams in similar conditions not a finance team in an ideal situation and a finance team in a very poor situation. The goal of the finance team in less ideal situations will be to rectify this situation. They can work on this by focusing on getting the unrestricted funding to be higher, this is a critical step. Some grants are primarily unrestricted, these are also great grants to have. The concept of unrestricted is not always so cut and dry, there is a lot of areas in the gray zone. If a donor does not have an attached budget to your funds, this would mean that these funds are closer to unrestricted. Some purists feel that unrestricted grants are only for those grants that would be fully unrestricted and allow one to create a surplus with these revenues, while this is the best type of unrestricted, other grants are functionally unrestricted as well even without the written approval to turn these funds into reserves. If the donor allows you to spend the funds as you wish, this is a great example of a major distinction point between unrestricted or not. If the donor does not allow you to spend as you wish but according to a strict budget, this falls into the restricted column.

## Sufficient Unrestricted Funds or Earned Revenue

Another major factor that is in line with the unrestricted versus restricted grant percentage is how much of your expenses are covered by restricted grants and how much are covered by unrestricted grants and how many expenses are not covered. The major issue here is having costs that are not covered by either a restricted or unrestricted grant. This situation can result from poor planning such as hiring staff that are unfunded, but with the expectation that the funding will come and it never does come. It can result from a donor leaving and no longer funding those expenses that were previously funded. The NPO must consider whether to close down this project or self-fund with the risk of creating a deficit. Hence, an organization that has gotten itself into this situation will face further obstacles. How will they fund these costs? Do they have reserves built up to cover these costs? How much reserves are left? And when does the reserve level get to a critical point?

This factor is similar to the situation where the NPO is not in a self-sustaining financial situation. This will take time and effort to correct. It will mean focusing on new grants that fund those specific unfunded costs or getting rid of those costs. There is also the ability to reallocate costs allocated to grants but this must be done very carefully and with full ethics. It is advisable to get donor clearance when something like this is undertaken. If expense X has been charged for the past four years and now they are being charged for expense Y, even if it falls into the same category, the donor may not appreciate being charged this cost without their approval or prior consent. It is crucial to treat the donors as your partners and not as if you are doing them a favor. In any NPO, the donor relationship is tantamount to success and they should be always treated fairly.

If a cost is to be moved from one project to another, certain rules must be followed, they can be summarized by the following:

**1. The cost should be directly related to the grant that is being charged**

**2. The grant should allow for this expense, explicitly or implicitly**

**3. The project manager of the grant must sign off that the expense is relevant and related to the project**

**4. It is important to consider the donor's reaction to such a change, would they fully support it or not?**

If the expense meets all of these criteria then it is fine to charge that expense. If there is any doubt whether the donor would approve this, it is wise to seek prior donor approval. If this is not done correctly and the donor finds out later and disapproves, this could have a significant negative reaction from the donor. That donor may no longer trust the NPO actions and this will make things worse for the NPO. It is always best to get input from the donor whenever there is any doubt. It is critical to keep your partners fully in the loop.

By following these rules, you will ensure that you maintain donor trust and by keeping a good dialogue with the donors you will be able to keep abreast of their needs.

In summary, the size of the finance team is a reflection of

the overall situation of the nonprofit, those in ideal situations can have relatively smaller teams, those in less ideal conditions will require a much bigger team, to achieve the same results.

# CHAPTER 8 - BUDGET, FORECASTING AND REPORTING

"THE FINANCIAL REPORT MAKES IT VERY CLEAR THAT IF WE GOT INTO HONEST BUDGETING TODAY, THAT IN FACT WE WOULD FIND OURSELVES WITH A MUCH LARGER DEFICIT THAN WE HAVE TODAY." - JIM COSTA

The budget, forecasting and reporting activities are critical to any organization whether it is a for-profit organization or a nonprofit. An organization can be a success or a failure based on this factor alone. If an entity is not able to set valid budgets for the upcoming year it will have little sense of the direction it should take. It will also not be good at evaluating where they are heading. Being able to know whether you are on track or off-target, in a timely manner, is critical. By knowing whether you are heading in the right path, one can stay on the current course and likely stay on course to success. If however, you are off the target and are not quickly aware of this issue, you will not be able to make the necessary adjustments promptly.

Creating your Budget is the first step in the process. This should be done before the start of the year and approved by the management team and the board. This should give a reliable picture of where you will be at the end of the year and what you can expect during the year. The budget should be achievable and reliable. If a budget is estimating $100 M of new revenue for the year, but new revenue has never been greater than $70 M, this is not a good situation unless there is a valid reason for this increase. Is there a donor that is very close to signing a very significant grant, that would lead to this sort of increase? Or is it more wishful thinking? Budgets should always be prepared with cautious and realistic optimism. The budget should be realistic and attainable. The approach followed should be consistent with prior years where a degree of reliability has been achieved. If the whole budget approach is changed and this results in a completely different budget level, it would make sense to review the reasonableness of this budget. A change in process may be called for, however, the process should not change the results unless the prior process was flawed. It is critical to consider the level of risk that the organization already has and the risk it is willing to take. An organization with a high degree of risk should be looking at offloading risk, while an organization in a very stable environment can decide to add risk, but this is at their discretion. An entity at a high risk situation that decides to take on more risk is foolhardy and may pay a serious price for this action.

### Difference in Budgeting in Nonprofits

One of the significant differences between a profit organization and a nonprofit organization is that for the most part, although not every case, the revenues in nonprofits are relatively small but high in frequency. If we look at Apple, the sale of the iPhone is relatively small compared to the size of the company, but they sell those in huge numbers throughout the year. In a nonprofit, the grants can average around $5 M, within a year they could have twenty or thirty of these transactions per year. The difference is very significant because, an additional donor or two could increase the funding level quite significantly, as well, a reduction by a few donors could have a significantly negative effect on operations. This makes it far more difficult to predict. If you sign one grant a month generally speaking, you could have a year where only 9 grants are signed or a year where 15 grants are signed. If we compare that to the sales of iPhones, Apple may sell thousands of these per day, let us assume their average is 10,000 per day, they would be expected to sell about 3.65 M units a year, it is very unlikely that they will sell only 1.0 M or that they will sell 5.5 M in the year. The range of sales for smaller items makes it far easier to estimate with larger numbers of sales. This makes budgeting in the nonprofit environment a lot more challenging.

Hence, predicting the amount of revenue coming from donors can be part science and part art. The best approach is to look at various scenarios. One may be the worst-case scenario, one may be a likely scenario and the other the best-case scenario. While planning the year, one should hope for the best but plan for the worse. One may have a scenario, wherein the worst case, the donors would be expected to sign $70 M of new contracts, while in the best case, they may sign $100 M or more. There is a significant difference between these two sums. This variance is not uncommon and could even be much greater. Once everyone has agreed with these three cases, best, likely and worst, the next step is to set a target. One may argue to choose the likely scenario and in many cases, this will be what is done. However, it is critical to understand the difference between the likely and worst-case scenarios. If the difference is $15 M, let us assume the likely scenario is $85 M. The best way to make a decision on which target to aim for is to look at the consequences of aiming for a higher figure but only achieving a lower amount. For example, if the entity is to expect $85 M and let us say they only receive $70 M, how much deficit will this cause. Let us assume a 50% loss rate, hence, this could incur a $7.5 M deficit. The loss rate could be lower, about 33%, which would result in a $5 M deficit. This figure could have a very negative effect on the reserves. If the reserves are very significant, then this will not be much of an issue, but if they are very small, the entity should not be taking these additional risks and should aim for the worst-case scenario in all instances. Hence, before the start of each year, the entity must choose the budget that they are satisfied with and understand what level of risk would be acceptable.

## Use Recent History

The most recent years will be an indicator of acceptable risk. If the organization has had many years of surplus in a row and a very healthy surplus level, then they are in a position to take on more risk. Taking on additional risk can be a good thing, it can allow you to start funding a project before it is funded by a donor and this would give an advantage in terms of funding and being able to position themselves much better. There will also be less start-up time as they have already taken the first few steps. It is critical to understand that this approach should only be taken where the risks are manageable and where the surplus is very strong, hence, any loss will not create much of an issue. An NPO should not risk losses where a loss could or would create an issue, this would be too risky and poor management.

## Forecasting

After having a very strong budget, it is critical to have a strong forecasting system in place. This may even be more critical than the budget process. A good forecasting system will allow you to know at any point during the year, whether you are on target or off-target. In many institutions, this process is done simply by taking the current spend and prorating it over the year. The problem with this is that during the year, it is very uncommon to have a consistent and stable spending rate. There may be higher costs in certain months and lower costs in others. Taking these factors into account is critical, to putting a good forecast system in place. Being able to make valid and correct decisions can only be done by having a strong forecasting system in place. In one organization, there was a poor forecasting system in place, that just prorated the current expense over the year. With this they were expecting a surplus, however, the reality was that they were heading towards a deficit. This was due to simply prorating the actual costs, when in fact there were costs that were building up but were not yet charged. In this situation, the entity should have been putting on the brakes, they were instead pressing the gas to spend more. In the end, they were warned in time to adjust, but not before speeding up spending and then hitting the brakes very hard on spending.

Their forecasting system was replaced by a much stronger system of forecasting and the results were spectacular. Management knew when they could spend or when they needed to hold back, this change had a dramatic and positive effect throughout the entire organization.

A strong forecasting system must be in place and must be reliable. The next step is that the results of these forecasts must be made on a timely basis and shared with all management so that any needed mitigation steps could be effected swiftly.

## Not Difficult
It is not that difficult to do right, but it is very easy to do this wrongly. Any finance team should be able to deliver a strong forecast to management. Some simple steps can ensure a good process. It is important to take note that certain items may be very hard to predict and this should be taken into account with any given forecast, but there are other areas which should be very easy to forecast. As an example, forecasting for a project that is already ongoing should be very simple and one should have a very strong estimate of the revenues and costs involved, while on the other hand, a project that is not yet signed would be very difficult to estimate whether it will be funded or not. Hence, a good approach is to have a budget and forecast for signed grants and then a separate one for potentially signed or expected to be signed, One may expect to sign an additional $10 M in grant revenue during the first three months and perhaps this would be for a two-year grant, hence, if that grant is

signed, it could result in a spend of $2.5 M, but if not signed, it will result in no additional spend. This is where the budgeting and forecasting can get a bit more of an estimation and perhaps less scientific. However, based on past experience one should reasonably be able to estimate the volume of new grants expected to be signed each quarter. With that being said, it will still be difficult to know which new grants will be signed.

### Reporting

The reporting should be timely, reliable, understandable and actionable to be effective. If a report is delivered too late, then it may not be that useful and if it is not reliable, this may be even worse. It may contain the correct information but if not reliable, it does not matter as it will not be relied on to make any decisions. Forecasts and budgets must be highly reliable. This way decisions can be made with confidence.

With a strong forecasting and reporting system in place, an organization will be able to make changes to their business to be able to get back on track or to stay on track, as necessary. This alone can be the difference between a well-run organization and a poorly run organization. This would assume that management makes the correct decisions and that the entity is overall a going concern.

An added complication with a nonprofit is that it is possible to be spending at the right budget overall and still incurring a deficit. This can happen if you are underspending on your restricted grants but overspending on your unrestricted grants. If this were to continue, you will overspend on your unrestricted grants, which means you will incur a deficit and you will be underspending on your restricted grants which do not result in a gain, hence, overall you will have a net deficit. This deficit may be considered a temporary deficit, if you can overspend on your restricted grants in the following year, hence, catch up to your spend target and then underspend on your unrestricted grants. But, this catching up is not that likely, unless the sum is quite minimal. Hence, it is best to avoid these situations. If you are certain that it is an issue that can be corrected in one year, then this is fine, but do not allow it to go beyond one year. With a strong reporting system and a management team that addresses these issues, these issues can be resolved before they even become problematic.

## Key Performance Indicators

With any good reporting system, there should be a critical number of key performance indicators (KPI) to track every month to ensure that everything is going as planned. This report should have all the key performance indicators necessary to ensure the financial health of the institution. It should be sent every month and on a timely basis to all management. Should there be any key performance indicator that is lagging this should be reviewed and corrections should be sought. The CEO and CFO should both oversee this task. The financial health of the organization cannot be properly managed without a strong cooperation between the CFO and CEO.

# CHAPTER 9 - GRANTS DIVISION

T he grants division is a critical function in any nonprofit but many individuals attribute the ability to sign new grants or lack thereof and attribute that to the grants division. This is a very common misunderstanding of what the team can and cannot achieve. The ability to sign more grants is far more connected with the nonprofits' ability to drive results, much more than the ability of the grants divisions fundraising abilities. Hence, blaming the grants division on a decrease in the signing of new grants is not a valid assignment of blame. Yes, a grants division can make some mistakes and if they do, they can cause the loss of a grant, but generally, they operate at a normal level and decrease is a sign of two things, either a general decline in the market or a decline in the nonprofit's ability to drive results. Neither of those two has anything to do with the actions of the grants division or team.

**Possible Reporting Lines**
There are many possibilities for the reporting line of the Grants Division, one may be to the CEO another would be to the CFO, and perhaps another to the COO. In many cases, it may depend on the personalities involved, but overall the most efficient reporting line would be through the CFO. The reason is that the two best people to be able to forecast the future revenues of

the organization would be the head of the grants team or fund-raising team and the CFO.

For the CFO to be effective in their role, they must have access to the amount of likely revenue coming in through the grants team. The best way to achieve this is through a direct reporting line. In some cases, an indirect reporting line would also work, but it is less efficient than the person and function reporting directly to the CFO.

## Division of Expertise

Often the head of the fundraising team is very good at their main function which is fundraising, but not always that great with financial reporting. By having this person report to the CFO, this issue can be resolved and the CFO can put the information from this division in a manner that is easy to follow and more reliable. There may be a tendency for the grants person to be very positive about the possibilities of a grant, while the CFO will usually look at both sides and come up with a more achievable conclusion. The CFO will be able to see the big picture and not just the revenue side. Hence, they will have a better understanding of the effects of being overly optimistic when it comes to potential funding. For this reason, the CFO will better understand when a conservative approach is called for and what the risks are for an overly optimistic approach.

## CEO and Finance

Most very good CEOs understand finance very well, but even from those very few understand it to the level that their CFO understands finance. This is to be expected, as it is not their job to cover finance. It is their job to run the organization and with a strong CFO who manages the financial future of the organization while reporting to the CEO or to the board. The CEO may want to have the head of funding report directly to them, this is understandable as they would like to have first access to the information. However, this approach is the wrong approach.

What generally occurs with this approach is the CFO is missing vital information for them to feed that back to the CEO and the management team, in general. A much better approach is to have the person report directly to the CFO and there could be an indirect reporting line to the CEO. This approach is the most efficient and ensures the needs of all are covered. The opposite occurs on some occasions where the function reports directly to the CEO and indirectly to the CFO, this does not work, as the CFO reports directly to the CEO and this will cause confusion.

This team is critical to the success of the NPO. If they cannot raise funds and do not have their own source of earned revenue, then an NPO must be able to raise funds each year to fund their operations. The vast majority of nonprofits require a significant amount of fundraising each year to be viable. The other way is the exception rather than the rule. Due to this critical role, they sometimes report directly to the CEO. Another reason for this is the success of a CEO can be measured by how much revenue they can raise and continue to raise.

## The CEO must be able to Raise Donor Contributions

A nonprofit or a CEO that cannot raise donor funds will have a challenging time, to say the least. It is a significant role of the CEO to be able to steer the NPO in such a way to ensure that donors feel confident that they will achieve the results that are expected. If a CEO cannot deliver that level of trust and respect with the donors, then they will suffer in their role and worse the NPO will suffer. Many things can go well or poorly but at the end of the day, if the donor fundraising efforts are yielding positive results then that is a very positive sign for the CEO and their management. If, on the other hand, the fundraising efforts have been declining for years, this is a clear indication that the donors have lost trust with the CEO and with the nonprofit. At the end of the day, if the NPO does not have its own source of funds, and most do not, then a true measure of success would be its fundraising abilities. If an NPO cannot raise funds and its fundraising efforts yields less and less funds each year, this is a bad sign for both the CEO and the NPO.

Should an NPO be in the position of having several years of declining fundraising efforts and no valid reason to justify the decline in fundraising, this would show a very significant weakness. There could not realistically be a justifiable position for having more than two or three years of sustained poor results in fundraising. There could be a decline for one to two years due to a recession in the global economy, this could account for about two years, perhaps during the 2008 - 2009 period, but no longer than that. Perhaps if the issue is resolved, this could account for this issue. For example, if the nonprofit was fighting AIDS and the disease was cured overnight, this may result in the entity facing sharp declines in funding, but this situation is almost unheard of. A war could affect the region that they are working in and make operations almost impossible. This would be a valid reason, but this situation would likely cause an increase in fundraising, while at the same time a halting of operations. It is unlikely to cause a reduction in fundraising. The issue would be front and center and countries would be pleased to contribute to help aid the people in this war-torn country.

## Likely cause of Decline in Fundraising

The reality is that the most likely cause of a general, significant and sustained reduction in funding can only be caused by one reason and that would be the donors are not in agreement with the CEO or they do not trust the CEO and the path that the NPO is now on. No person can please everyone all the time and donors will come and go, but a true test of success is that more donors will come to the table than leave. Hence, you are either maintaining or gaining, not losing donor funding. Can a CEO who faces this situation of a sustained reduction in funding, correct it? It is very difficult to do so. There is something about the CEO that caused that situation, in the first place. The likelihood of them being able to change the way that they have operated for many years or decades is very slim. One could think that the donors just do not like the CEO and it is for this reason that they are no longer funding the NPO. This may occur in a very few situations, but the reality is most donors are not that fickle, they are looking at expected results versus known costs and whether they feel the entity is trustworthy and on the right track, this is far more important than personalities.

The day to day operations of the NPO will affect the fundraising. Hence an NPO that is delivering strong results with modest funding will be seen as a very good investment. This is the key to success and one of the most important principles for success. It is important to have good fundraisers, but at the end of the day, you are selling results and impact. A donor who believes that you will deliver the best bang for the buck and who is aligned with your mandate is a donor that is very likely to fund you. It is sometimes the case that an NPO may look to hire strong fundraisers with the idea of getting more revenue in, this may help in the short run, but the reality is that no matter who is fundraising for you if you are not cost-effectively delivering results or you are not aligned to the donor's goals, you will not likely get funding from that donor. If the donor does not trust or buy into your methodology or strategy, you will have an almost impossible time to get funding from that donor.

### Ways to increase Funding

The CEO has two effective ways to increase donor funding, the first is they should ensure the results delivered are strong and real. It is very easy for any NPO to say that they have delivered strong results, but those that can demonstrate this through third parties are the ones that will be more believable. The other thing that they must do is meet directly with their major donors and partners to ensure the future funding of the organization. If the CEO cannot demonstrate efficiency in operations and a record of achieving results, they will have a very difficult time raising funds. The more you have to "sell", then it is likely the worse you are doing. If your results speak for itself, then fundraising will be the least of your concerns. Hence, it makes sense that the primary role of a CEO of an NPO is to drive results at the lowest cost. This efficiency will result in better fundraising results. If the CEO cannot demonstrate efficiency in results or worse shows a worsening picture for results, they will have a very difficult time in fundraising and donors will feel that their money is not going as far as in the past. The donors will likely look to use their funds elsewhere.

It is a common thing that when fundraising is failing, there is blame placed on the fundraisers. The reality is that the true person responsible for raising funding of the NPO is the CEO and their success in managing the entity will result in increased funding, just as any failures will result in decreased fundraising. A good fundraising team can help improve a good situation or even a decent situation, but a great fundraising team cannot be effective when results are declining or there is a loss of donor confidence. At the end of the day, if your end product is not strong, it will be difficult to sell.

From a finance perspective the donor team should be able to tell what grants are there and what grants are about to expire but most importantly, the donor team, in coordination with the finance team, must come up with a strong estimate of the likely contracts to be signed during the year. This will allow finance to give good estimates to base their likely spend and revenue targets.

## Active Agreements

A grants team will have a list of active signed agreements. This should form the majority of the spending for the year. This part or the equation is simple for both the grants team and the finance team. The next more complex area is the new funding in the year, in other words, which of the grant proposals will be likely signed and at which approximate date. If a grant is signed on January 1st then there will be a full year of operations, while if signed on December 31st, there will be no operations during the year. Hence, not only is it important to know which grants have a strong likelihood of being signed, but it is also important to have an idea of the date by which they are expected to be signed. This should be supplied by the funding or donor team and reviewed by the finance team. The finance team can use the past few years and look at the overall real rate of results given by the donor team. As an example, if the donor team has a habit of always being overly optimistic with regards to the likelihood of grants being signed, the finance team can factor that in. I have seen this approach many times, and many donor teams seem to be overly optimistic about what can be signed. If there is a pool of proposals that accounts for $100 M of grants, the donor team may feel each has an average of 20% likelihood of being signed, this would equate to $20 M additional business, if however, the real rate is closer to 10%, they would have overestimated this by $10 M. This can have a significant and negative effect.

## Budgeting and Forecasting

When it comes to budgeting and forecasting, these two should be treated differently. Hence, the first stage would be the existing grants and one could assume there will be no new contracts signed during the year, this could represent the worst-case scenario and also, for the most part, the guaranteed minimum, since the grants are already signed. Then the next two scenarios could be the expected grants to be signed, and an optimistic view of this sum. Hence, the realistic view would be the sum of what is already signed and what is likely to be signed. Then the optimistic view would be what is already signed plus the amount expected to be signed from an optimistic perspective. In the ideal situation, the likely amount should be mid-way between the minimum or pessimistic view and the optimistic view. Hence, if your minimum funding level is $80 M and your likely funding level is $90 M, then your optimistic view should be about

$100 M, this would not make sense to have an optimistic view of $150 M or $200 M, if your minimum is $80 M and your likely is $90 M.

Now that you have set a likely amount of fundraising for the year, you should now look to report on that, hence, if they are to raise another $10 M for this year, this would mean that on average $1 M must be signed per month for the current year.

It is important to note that the average duration of a donor agreement is not one year, but it can be anywhere from one year to five years, with an average of about three and a half years. For simplicity's sake, let us assume the average is four years. It is important to look at the age of your grants and see how many are expiring this year or next year. Ideally, your grants should be staggered, such that each year roughly 25% of your grants are expiring and you do not see one year where 100% of your grants expire. If your average spend per year is $100 M, this means that you should be on average signing $100 M per year on new grants, assuming that 100% of your funding comes from grants. If 90% comes from grants then you should be looking to find new funding for $90 M per year. This amounts to $7.5 M per month. You also want to take into account inflation and general growth, so you should be looking to increase your average every year. If you sign a five-year grant for $20 M, then that will equate to $4 M per year if signed in June, then half of one year, or $2 M, would increase this year's budget.

### CFO Involvement

The CFO must be directly involved in the management of this information. It is for this reason that a clear and direct reporting line to the CFO is crucial for good management and efficiency. For the CEO, it would make sense to have an indirect reporting line from that role as well.

It is also important to note that the fundraising ability of this team can only be as good as the results that have been delivered by the NPO as a whole. This function, the delivery of results, is more related to the role of the CEO. Possibly the most critical function is raising funds in an NPO and this is tied to the overall delivery of impact or overall effectiveness, which can only be the result of the CEO. Ultimately, the CEO is responsible for good results and also responsible for poor results. Hence, should there be a year where funding has dropped or several years, it is more likely due to the poor performance of the CEO than the poor performance of the fundraising team. There are some major errors this team can make and that could be a cause for a decrease in funding, but we will assume that they are doing their job at a reasonable level. Hence, they are meeting deadlines for donor reporting and ensuring the proposals get to the right people at the right time. Often the fundraising teams are blamed for poor results, this is incorrect, the reason for poor results in fundraising is directly linked to the overall performance of the NPO which is often linked to the performance of the CEO and the Board.

Overall this function is critical and there should be an oversight from both the CFO and CEO, however, it is more efficient if the CFO has a more direct role in managing the team and function, while the CEO should focus more on the operational side of matters. In general, it would make good sense for the CFO to cover the whole admin process and the CEO to cover the whole of operations. While the CFO would also report to the CEO or to the Board, hence, they would cover the whole function. This way the CEO can focus their time on ensuring the operations are getting results, while the CFO can ensure that the whole admin function runs smoothly. From time to time, the CEO will need to work directly with the fundraising teams and hence, there is a logic for an indirect reporting line.

This area is often misunderstood in most nonprofits. Often the fundraising teams are blamed for poor performance in fundraising which has little to do with their work and they often report directly to the CEO or the equivalent of this position.

# CHAPTER 10 -
# FUNDING MODELS

There are two main types of funding models, one is creating a fund and the other is going after funding each year. The primary distinction between these two is with the fund approach the idea is to have revenues from the fund that sustains the operations. In this regard, the fund is operational without the need to go back to the donors each year. Ideally, the passive income from the fund now pays for the annual operations of the organization.

For the fund model, one requires a very significant one-time contribution from donors and the other model requires smaller but annual contributions from donors. If on average an organization can earn a 5% return on funds and estimates an annual cost of $10 M, then to fund this in perpetuity the donors would need to come up with $200 M, then from this, they can come up with their annual expenses of $10 M per year and no further request from donors is required. The challenge with this is that it is far more difficult to raise $200 M than it is to raise $10 M. If their annual spend is $100 M, then funding a $2 B fund would be required, not an easy task.

**Fund Approach**

While it is more difficult to get to the fund approach, any non-profit should aim to develop a hybrid approach. One can request funding as a fund contribution, that the entity can only spend on the revenues generated from that grant. The other thing that should be looked at is creating this fund from your unrestricted funding or any reserves developed over the years. If you have fully unrestricted funds of $5 M per year, this amount should go to your reserves and you should be looking at investing these funds in stocks and bonds that can earn a minimum of 5% per year. After four years, you will have over $20 M in your port-folio and now you will be earning a minimum of $1 M per year. These funds would be completely unrestricted. They should also complement your reserves to earn more funding. If your portfolio doubles every ten years within thirty years you will now have a significant sum in your reserves and you will be earning a significant amount of revenues which will get you the financial stability that is needed. Ideally, any nonprofit that has been in business for over twenty or thirty years should be well down this path. This concern for long term sustainability is ne-cessary to bring into the equation of every strategy, the issue is that most do not do this and this leaves the NPO very vulner-able to swings in funding levels.

## Surpluses should be viewed Positively

Donors must not interpret "profits" or "surpluses" as a negative, these are necessary elements to financial sustainability. This is also a necessity to allow organizations to pass through difficult periods. If one year the funding drops by 10%, then the revenues on these funds could make up that difference, leaving the entity to be far more sustainable and less chaotic in their spending rates. If the spend rate had to match exactly the funding rate of each organization, this would result in a very chaotic spend rate with lots of hires and fires throughout the years. This is nei-ther ideal nor sustainable. Where this could get to be a problem is that if the fund ballooned to such a large size that it could be seen as an abuse of funding. If the funding does get larger, it is important to use the funding wisely, one area that is always underfunded is capital assets. Are the buildings in need of repair, how old is the fleet and how are they being maintained. Are there new project areas on the horizon and do they need a head-start to get them on their way.

All nonprofits should strive to have 25% of your annual spend come from earned income, this cannot be achieved overnight but it should be a goal. It may take decades to reach this goal, but each nonprofit should be moving towards that goal and not away from that goal. Most nonprofits are nowhere near this amount. If you estimate that your return is likely safe at 5%, then you would need to have five times your annual spend in reserves to achieve this level of earned income. If your goal is to have 100% of your spend funded by earned passive income, one would require 20 times your annual spending. Hence, if your annual spending is roughly $ 100 M, you would need $ 2 B in your reserves. This is not an easy thing to achieve, but it is achievable and some have done it.

### How to Build a Fund

One approach is you could start fundraising for the fund directly itself. You could request that donors fund directly to the fund or a percentage of your funding to the fund. One possibility is that for every dollar funded, then 15% goes to the admin costs and 10% goes to the fund. This will have the effect of requiring less funding down the road. It will not be easy to accomplish but it never hurts to ask. There is also a rising concern among some donors that they are not funding the full cost and some are funding less than the full costs which harms the NPO. They understand that this hurts the long term stability of an organization, but some organizations will take the funding in any case and some are forced to do so, in order to limit their losses.

It takes good financial management and good overall management which can be delivered by a solid Chief Executive

Officer, a strong CFO, and a good board who understand the importance of these things in the long run, but in many cases, they are not even considered and this can be seen by the number of long-standing charities that do not have a significant portion of their funding being self-funded. In the ideal situation, about 25% - 50% would come from self-funding. This would allow the institution freedom to self-fund projects they prefer and to save for capital projects down the road. At the point when the fund can fund 5% - 10% of your operations, this is already a significant step forward and the entity is well on its way to getting to the next step. The first step is to get to 5%, which would require having a year of spending in reserves. This small step can have a significant effect on stability and overall operations. For this to occur, one needs to save a minimum of one year in reserve and also invest that sum in a vehicle where a stable return of 5% or more can be achieved with little risk.

## Gain in Efficiency

Once you reach a 25% to 50% range, this would yield a huge advantage in terms of self-sufficiency, financial stability, and overall funding. If we take the example of 25%, hence, imagine your annual operations of $100 M, then you are now at the point where your investment income is $25 M per year, if one is averaging 5% on the market this would mean that you would need a fund of $500 M, this is a significant sum, especially considering that the average annual spend is $100 M, this means that you are holding five years of reserves to get 25% of your funding through investment income. While this may seem impossible to achieve, it is not impossible. It does require two things, the first is a proper strategy to get there and full disclosure to the donor partners of the benefits in doing so. If 5% - 10% of your savings can be stored into your reserves, which is possible and your reserves are earning a growth rate of somewhere between 5% - 10%, this can be achieved within thirty years or less.

The higher this percentage is the less efforts that must be

directed towards fundraising and the less dependence on donor funding there would be. This would allow an entity to make choices with regards to their infrastructure and with regards to choosing projects that may be difficult to fund for one reason or another through a traditional donor approach.

## Financial Success

The financial success of an organization can be seen as how much progress is made on this front. With the success of any good nonprofit organization one must consider two main aspects, their impact, I.e the good that they do and their financial sustainability. It is of no use, doing good but being bankrupt in two years, just as it is of no use, having a significant funding base but not able to deliver positive results. These two principles of delivering results and financial health are two of the most important principles of all nonprofits.

A small improvement in earned income can have a significantly positive effect on the overall operations of a nonprofit.

# CHAPTER 11
# - METRICS &
# EVALUATION

**M**etrics & Evaluation (M&E) is an important topic concerning nonprofits. In profit organizations it is far simpler to see success, success is often viewed as the bottom line and one can see the income statement and right away determine if there is any success or not. If there are profits then there is success, this is very simple to see.

### Measuring Success in a Nonprofit

With a nonprofit it is very different, for the most part, there will be no income or no surplus. The accounting is set up that for the most part the expenditures and revenues match. Hence, this is not a good tool to use for evaluating the results of an entity. The best way to value the work of an entity is to look at their metrics & evaluation (M&E) reports. When we speak of M&E we are generally looking at outputs, outcomes, and impact. The outputs are directly related to the costs of a project, so if project X delivered five pieces of training in Bangladesh, the output would be those five pieces of training. There is then the outcome from those five pieces of training, perhaps during those five trainings 100 participants were trained, this would be the results or the outcomes. Then what those people, in turn, do with those results would be the impact. The output and outcomes are much easier to report, while the impact needs more time to measure. Let us say that the training is geared towards AIDS to reduce the rate of incidence. The training will go to trainers who will train more and also disseminate knowledge. If those five trainings trained 100 trainers, and these went on to disseminate knowledge and train others, over a year, they could then look at the incidence of AIDS and see that it dropped to 3%. One could then make the argument that the incidence rate dropped due to this training. This is where attribution plays a role, it could be that the slowing in the rate was 100% because of the training, but it also could be that the training had very little effect on this drop. Perhaps this drop was due to the people at risk becoming more saturated and hence new cases would be less. It could be that another NGO was offering free protection against AIDS. This is where attribution is complex. What is needed to see is what happens in similar environments where the training did not take place. Hence, if you could know exactly what the rate would have been without giving the training, then you could know what your impact was. If the rate without the training would have been 5% and with the training, it was only 3%, then and only then, can you fully attribute the results to this training. While attribution may seem simple, with all the factors that change in any given environment, the change is not always evident. While it is difficult, it does not mean that efforts should not be made to estimate this. The efforts should be made but the accuracy must be taken with a grain a salt unless there are strong comparators where the data shows no significant change. If you have two very similar villages and one you offer the training and the other you do not, then you notice that the one with the training had a 3% incidence rate but the one without the training had a 5% incidence, assuming there were no other factors, one could conclude that the reduction was due to the training.

When looking at the efficiency of any project, one must look at the costs and compare it with the output, expected out-comes and expected impact. It must be clear that the output is relative to the costs, this would be the first critical step. For example, a donor may not appreciate spending $1 M for the output of one training class that can train up to ten people. This would not have the appropriate value for the amount of spend. If it were to hold 1,000 training events and each would have about 100 people being trained, then it could have value. Spending $10 per person getting trained is quite good value for money, but spending $100,000 per person getting trained would not be worth it and no donor would pick up this project. The people getting trained is not sufficient though, there must be some impact of those people being trained. If it can be shown that these people being trained can now reduce poverty in their region by applying this training, then this could have a signifi-cant impact in a region and the price being paid could be seen as reasonable. For a donor to pick up the funding of a project, the impact must be aligned to their goals and strategic plan. If their focus is on reducing the incidence rate of AIDS in Africa, then there may be a great project in Asia to reduce poverty, but it will not be aligned with their objectives. They may want to keep the project on file and save it for a later date when their priorities line up there. Each donor has different priorities and knowing which donors have matching priorities to your project is a key to success. If the priorities are aligned and the donor can see good value in your proposal and has trust that the figures and impact estimate is reasonable, then there is a good likelihood for success, unless there is another project with better results and better trust from the donor.

Donor trust is a key component of fundraising. A donor may like or may not even like a given project team, but they still may fund it in either case. Donor trust is another story, if a donor does not trust an entity, for whatever reason, they will go out of their way not to fund them and may even decide to pull their funding prematurely. There are two areas where a donor can lose trust in an NPO, one would be overestimating impact and results and then under-delivering on those promises. This would be the case where a project promises certain outcomes and impacts but falls very short of these estimations. This would mean that the donor spent funds with certain expectations but the expectations fall very short of meeting them. This is a bad reputation to have with any donor, as you may have a good project but if the donors do not believe that you can deliver on your expected results, then it will not be believable and they would prefer to go with another entity that has delivered well on their promises. Another area to lose trust with a donor is on financial reporting. If the financial reporting uses very unusual accounting practices or charges costs that do not belong to the donor, this could result in a total lack of financial trust for a given donor. There will be little chance of getting additional funding with that donor and it is a very good possibility that they may cancel all grants with you immediately. This is an area that should never be played with. There is no reason to risk this. This could result in very swift and negative consequences for the institution. I would always advise that it is better to check with your donor before charging an amount where any uncertainty to the validity of that charge exists.

**End Goal**

With M&E the end goal would be a strong measurement of results, along the lines of output, outcomes and impact and a very reliable system for predicting outcomes and impact for ongoing and future projects. It is important to have a great system to measure the actual results but also a great system to estimate future results. The estimation of results will play a positive role in the reliability of future projects and thus have a positive effect on their ability to be funded. You want to set up projects that can deliver great results and have an impact that is aligned with the donors' strategy. A strong M&E team will be able to provide reasonable estimates of the expected outcomes and impact. This reasonable estimate is a cornerstone to the success of a project and the more successful projects you have the more successful the NPO is. It is surprising that the M&E team remains relatively understaffed and often they are missing the required expertise. A strong M&E function is necessary to ensure strong results, you need to be able to measure when you are succeeding or not succeeding in order to be successful.

## Monetization of Results

Another goal of M&E, but one that I have not seen achieved yet, in a reliable manner, is the monetization of output, outcomes, and impact. If there was a strong way that we could reliably measure the results intrinsically but also attach a reliable monetary figure to, this would be a major improvement on how we measure results. Let us take the example previously mentioned if we look at our output - having 1,000 training events, our outcomes are having 100,000 people trained and our impact is a reduction of AIDS incidence of 1% (assume a population of 1,000,000). Imagine if the monetary value of holding a training is $200 and imagine the value of training a person is $5 and lastly the saving of a person not having AIDS is $500. We could sum of all the output, outcomes and impact and get a value of $1,000 times 500 or $500,000 for the output, the people being trained would have a value of $5 times 100,000 or $500,000 and the valuation of the impact would be $200 times 1,000,000 times 1% or $2,000,000, the total sum of all would be $3,000,000 and this divided by the costs would give a 3 to one ratio. This would be a great project for funding. It is important to note that the valuation is not measured as improvement in life but in the cost of achieving this result elsewhere. For example, supplying medicine to prevent aids for 100 people, may prevent AIDS for 20 people and that may reasonably cost $2,000, hence, the savings would be measured in this way. The actual saving of a life would be hard to give a monetary figure to but would be far greater and many thousand times greater than the magnitude in this example.

The challenge, of course, is putting reasonable figures to value the output, outcome, and impact. While this is difficult to do, it is also not so difficult to find a reasonable range of values that could be agreed upon. Every donor does this each time they look into a project. They are intrinsically evaluating what is the overall results expected and what impact will it likely have versus how much it will cost. If the estimated value does not exceed the costs, they will not fund the project. Every donor also has limited resources and they would like the most results for a given price. This is a critical measurement of success of an NPO, if you can deliver value for money, I.e achieve a high impact that is significantly more valuable than the costs to attain them, then this will drive up your ability to fund more projects and attain more success.

**M&E is required for Success**
Overall, M&E plays a key role in the success of an organization and one area that is unfortunately overlooked in many institutions. The importance of M&E is as critical as the finance side, with every new grant proposal, there must be a proper estimate of budgets, but as well, there must have a proper estimate of M&E. The M&E team should review the estimates within projects and see that it is in line with the budget estimates and ensure that it is attainable. It is also important to ensure that the results can be measurable and attributable. If there are issues with these, the M&E estimates should contain notes to explain any potential difficulties in measurement or attribution. It is better to provide warnings in advance than give a warning later, that the M&E will be hard to collect and verify.

A strong M&E function is a key component to be able to ensure that an NPO that relies on donor funding can compete. Without a strong M&E function, both the proposals will have less of a chance of being funded, but also the measurements of results will fall short of expectations. This means that projects that have a poor realization of results will not be highlighted and those projects with strong results will also not be highlighted. This will not allow teams to learn best practices and to learn from areas that were not successful. There are many things to learn from failures and many things to learn from successes, without a strong M&E function, this learning will not occur. As well, strong success stories would not be highlighted or used as an example. Just as equally, there would be no explanation given to poorly performing projects, which will leave the donor unsatisfied and will result in less trust.

Putting efforts into M&E and having a department that works and is reliable is a critical function in the nonprofit world. One has to remember that the donors are giving funds, not for the sake of spending money but to get some impact and results. The donor and the nonprofit must be able to evaluate and present the results of M&E during a project, after completion of a project and in some cases, after a significant time has passed after the closing of a project. This function is critical to success, just as a strong function of donor reporting, fundraising, project teams, and a strong finance unit are key components to ensuring a strong future for any nonprofit.

### More Resources needed in M&E

The M&E team is one of the best teams to determine the success or lack of success of projects and hence, is critical to the overall success of the nonprofit. However, many nonprofits do not put the proper resources into this function and thus lose any potential benefits of having a strong M&E function.

# CHAPTER 12 - INTERNATIONAL FINANCIAL REPORTING STANDARDS

B efore the advancements of IFRS, each country developed its own Generally accepted accounting Policies, GAAP. While many had similarities, others were quite different. Some Country's GAAP put a preference on the Balance sheet, like US GAAP, while others put a preference on the income statement like Canada GAAP and UK GAAP.

This did not pose a problem for decades until as globalization got more advanced and more common, it became clear that the different reporting standards meant understanding the Financial Statements from a different perspective.

## US GAAP
Due to the size of their economy, the US GAAP played an im-

portant role, however, other GAAPs like Canada and the UK, since they were based on the income statement as opposed to the balance sheet seemed to have an advantage, in terms of relevance. In the 1970's it was agreed by many countries to look into this issue and start coming up with one approach. Many countries worked together in 1973 to form the International Accounting Standards Committee to harmonize these differences with the end goal of having one agreed set of accounting standards.

After over two decades had passed and without much progress, the G7 in 1998 requested this group to finalize a proposal by early 1999. The IASC then changes its Board and is replaced by the IFRS Foundation to continue this work. By the early 2000s, there was still some work to do to harmonize the US GAAP with IFRS. Most other GAAP's are far more similar to IFRS and hence the transition is not as difficult. The IFRS Board and FASB (US) adopt measures to accelerate this process of bringing the two standards closer together.

### Mid 2000's
By 2007, many countries have now signed on to the newly established IFRS. The US SEC allows non-US companies to report in IFRS and not in US GAAP. There is still some work on how to deal with US companies. Three options exist, keep reporting in US GAAP, allow a choice or force the US companies to adopt IFRS. In 2010, Canada bega using IFRS. Pressure is beginning to mount on other counties to follow suit and many do so. In 2014, China also agrees to transition to IFRS.

### Rules versus Policy Based
Another important distinction between US GAAP and IFRS is that the US GAAP has always been rules-based while IFRS is principles-based. Another way of looking at this is that whatever the situation is the US GAAP advocates for having a rule to account for that. While IFRS is based on a large number of widely accepted principles and the rules stem from those principles.

Professional judgement is required to move from the principles to its application. The challenge with the US GAAP is that the rules must be overly exhaustive to cover each variable or situation. While IFRS has principles that are used to figure out the financial treatment. Both have their pros and cons but having a streamlined process for determining how to treat a financial transaction would seem to have an advantage. In other words, the US GAAP must cover each likely and potential situation and then have a rule for that situation. While IFRS can reduce a lot of this by having an agreed principle. This principle is also one that has existed under many GAAPs before this change, such as Canadian and U.K. GAAP, both were based on principles and not rules. Again, making it easier for those countries to transition to IFRS. A major distinction between the rules-based approach and a principles-based approach is that with the principles-based approach you are required to use professional judgment to apply the principles to specific situations, whereas with the rules-based approach you primarily follow, look up, or memorize the rule.

As of today, there are more than one hundred countries that have either fully adopted or partially adopted IFRS. The US has still not adopted IFRS, but the goal of many is to also include the USA. While the US SEC does allow foreign companies to report in IFRS, it does not allow domestic companies to report in IFRS.

### Globalization

With globalization, it is clear that having one set of agreed-upon financial reporting standards is a good approach. Hence, the goal behind IFRS is positive and the progress is strong. It still needs to get over its largest hurdle and that is to get US adoption. It is unclear when or if this will ever occur. There will likely be some further negotiations and there will be a day where they will all agree on one approach, but we are still not that close to that day.

### Nonprofits and IFRS

How IFRS affects nonprofits is another complex area and not fully agreed to, as well. The accounting in most GAAPs all follow the matching principle. This principle is fundamental for accrual-based accounting as opposed to a cash basis of accounting. In simple terms, the matching principle allows for the recognition of revenue when it is earned and the recognition of expenses when they are incurred. While most nonprofits follow the same basis, some differ greatly on how this is applied to capital assets.

In many nonprofits rather than capitalizing long term assets and depreciating them over their useful life, they would expense them right away. This is a cash basis approach, in other words expensing the item once it is paid, which is not in accordance with the matching principle or the accrual basis of accounting. The proper method would be to capitalize the asset and expense it over time. If we take a car that costs $40,000 and has a useful life of ten years with no residual value. In accrual accounting, you would capitalize the full cost of that asset and then depreciate it by $4,000 each year. This way you are expensing the asset according to its useful life and following the matching principle and the accrual basis of accounting.

The reason this approach of expensing capital assets right away is used in accounting for some NPOs is that it is far simpler to have one set of books or accounting that can be applied to both the donor report and the internal financial statements. This may make it easier for donors to understand the financial statements and will ensure fewer variations. It is, however, against most GAAP and usually, this requires a qualification from the external auditors. In their opinion, they will state that the NPO follows GAAP except where it applies to the treatment of capital assets. This is very common and accepted by all parties, the NPO, the donors, the public, and the auditors.

One major change with IFRS is that it requires the recording of assets at fair value. This would result in a major change for most nonprofits. Imagine the case of a building that was donated to the NPO. If this building had a value of $5 M, then normally the full amount would have been expensed. Now, it will need to be recorded at fair market value, assuming this can be reasonably estimated. This change will be quite large, as now, they will not be in a position to write off the full amount as an expense on their books. This will dramatically change the revenues and the expenses of the NPO in that year.

It is, however, the correct approach. By using the old approach, the full amount of the building would have been recorded both as revenue and expense. This would result in a great rise in both revenues and expenses for that year and the subsequent year will likely see a decline for that amount. By using the accrual basis and IFRS, this spike in one year can be avoided. This is one of the benefits of the matching principle, it tends to reduce the levels of spikes in an income statement and smooths it over a longer period.

### Disadvantages of New Approach

The disadvantage of this new approach is that it will require to offset the asset with a liability. Hence, if a building is contributed and has a value of $5 M, this will require an asset with a value of $5 M, since the donor has paid for this it will also require a liability which would be unearned revenue. It is important to note that revenue can only be realized when earned. In the case of a restricted grant that is there for a purchase of a building, they would only be able to recognize the revenue once the expense was incurred, hence, each year when they recognize the depreciation expense there will also be a realization of the revenue and the unearned revenue liability will be decreased. In each subsequent year, there would be a write-down to the asset and the liability, as well, there would be an expense and a recognition of revenue. This would continue for the useful life of the asset.

The challenge here is that the treatment of that expense will be very different from the approached used with the donor. The donor report that is prepared by the nonprofit and delivered to the donor is not required to be prepared using full IFRS and it is not required to even fully use the accrual basis of accounting. Hence, for these types of reports, it could be acceptable that the donor agrees to the use of the cash basis approach for the treatment of assets. As such, in the donor report, the full cost of the building will show up as an expense and for external reporting purposes, there will be a capitalization of that cost and then amortization or depreciation over its useful life. This will result in a very large difference between the two reporting methodologies. Donors must understand this effect. If they are going to review the audited financial statements, this may show up as a large discrepancy. However, this difference is the proper way to treat the matter. Another approach would have the expense charged to the donor in the same manner, but this will require reporting to the donor for this asset for the next forty years or more. This would not be efficient for either the donor or the nonprofit, however, if the donor wishes this methodology to be the way to treat this, then the NPO should accommodate this request. If the NPO is fully against that concept, a discussion between the pros and cons can be held, but ultimately the donor will have the final say, as to which approach the NPO should use for the donor reporting, but not for the external reporting. The external reporting is handled by the NPO but reviewed by the external auditor to gauge an opinion as to the fairness of the financial statements and policies used to prepare them.

## IFRS not focused on Nonprofits

There is another issue with IFRS as it pertains to nonprofits, IFRS has stated that they have not completed the review for nonprofits and judgment should be used in their application. This is a very important issue. Many would like to use IFRS in the nonprofit community since many donor countries have already implemented IFRS or are well on their way to doing so. Hence, there is a desire with most donor countries with the USA as an exception to adopt IFRS as a standard. This makes very good logic, however, the challenge with this approach is that IFRS has not been adapted or prepared for nonprofits. One of the main elements of an IFRS system versus a US GAAP system is the focus on the income statement versus the balance sheet. With for-profit entities, this makes good sense. When you are looking at the valuation of a company the main thing that you are looking at is the likelihood of future profits and future growth. If an entity would never make a profit, then it should be valued at zero, this is the point where you would look at the valuation through the balance sheet. There are times when a company may have more value in assets than in future revenues. This would be a difficult situation as many may say to sell off the assets and close it down, this way you maximize the value of the underlying assets. There are far more points to consider before making a final decision. Most for-profits are in the position where their future profits are more than their equity and hence a valuation via the income statement makes sense and not through the balance sheet. This is why ultimately the income statement approach is better than the balance sheet approach and why most other countries follow an income statement philosophical approach and why the US GAAP is also changing towards that trend.

With nonprofits, the situation is quite different. The organizations do not have a value and are not traded on the stock exchange and they are nonprofits, hence, the idea of profit is not relevant. Thus, the logic that pushes the rationale for IFRS is less compelling in nonprofits. The income statement is useful to see growth trends in terms of revenue and expenses, but that is about it. While the balance sheet can play a far more critical role. Is the nonprofit financially healthy? Does it have a strong reserves balance? What are the types of assets other than cash that it carries? How liquid is the NPO? What is the balance of short term assets versus the balance of short term liabilities? By evaluating the balance sheet one will be able to discern the financial stability to some extent. The more reserves there are the more stable the nonprofit would be in general, especially important is the level of reserves compared to the annual average spend. Hence, an NPO that has reserves that are three times their average annual spending will be far more stable than one that has only half a year's worth of reserves.

## Recording at Fair Market Value

By recording things at fair market value, this is one area that the balance sheet approached is being used which may come at a cost to the income statement. As these changes in valuations each year may be great but the overall trend over a long period may be much smaller. Imagine an investment that one year gains $1 M and then the next year drops by $1 M and repeats this pattern. If IFRS is used, then there will be significant fluctuations in the income statement, while over a long period no change in the balance sheet. On the other hand, if this asset was recorded at cost and held at the lower of cost or market, then the income statement and balance sheet would not be affected each year. In this case, there is a trade-off. Recording the assets at fair market value is a good policy, however, by using this approach your income statements fluctuate greatly each year. On the other hand, if the value of an investment does rise and you are recording the asset at LCM or the lowest of cost and market value, then you will not adjust this cost for increases in value. This will allow you the ability to time your realization of gains by selling the asset when you decide. This may be used to cover a deficit. Hence, this also has some drawbacks. In the end, when we look at marketable securities, each approach has its pros and cons. Ultimately, the fact that the NPO or company could decide when to recognize its gain by selling is one that potentially could be abused. It may allow companies to recognize gains when it is convenient, despite that the gain may have occurred years ago. Hence, putting the assets at market value is a good policy. Perhaps a hybrid policy could be used where the company must state how long it is expected to hold the assets. The default may be 20 years, then any gains would need to be amortized over 20 years, but the next years' losses or gains will affect the following years' allocation. This would have the effect of recording some of the gain or loss each year, but not the full gain or loss in one year. Over time, much of the gain or loss would be incorporated into the company. This could be a hybrid approach to LCM and valuing at market value. It would protect the income statement from wild fluctuations and allow the balance sheet to present the full market value in the notes. Any sales before the 20 year period needs to be amortized, this will ensure that the company avoids selling short term gains or short term losses to modify their income. Another approach would be to take out this type of income altogether. There is no easy answer with this one, but it is clear that the current recommendation does have some issues to iron out.

As IFRS for nonprofits has not been fully ironed out yet and fully agreed upon, there are some areas where judgment is left to the NPO. Currently, as a nonprofit transitions from US GAAP to IFRS one very critical area that is left as a choice is whether assets are to be recorded at cost or written off. Since the policy has not been finalized, they have left that as an option for the nonprofit. This area could also cause a lot of friction between various nonprofits.

### Some Choices for Treatment in IFRS
The reason for this choice is most likely because forcing the NPOs to adopt the IFRS policies would be a very large charge for the processes of many NPOs. On the other hand, having one process would reduce any ambiguity and allow for better comparisons across different NPOs. There could be confusion on how the reporting would work, where their reporting for both the donor and the NPO must be the same, but this is not necessarily true. The NPO could still follow the policy of accrual basis of accounting and capitalize the asset and amortize it over its useful life, while, at the same time prepare a donor report based on the cash basis with respect to the treatment of capital assets.

Donor reports just like tax returns do not have to fully follow IFRS or US GAAP. For many countries, some expenses are invalid for tax purposes but valid for accounting purposes or there may be different ways to calculate depreciation. Taxes may allow for a quicker write off of the asset, allowing a savings of tax, while accounting policies would not allow for that quick depreciation of these assets. You would not prepare your fiscal expenses according to how you fill in your tax return. The same is true for a donor report. It would be completely valid to fully expense a capital asset for your donor report and then on your financial statements, these are capitalized. The donor would be fully aware of any large discrepancies that may exist between how expenses are handled within the donor reports and how these same expenses would be treated for accounting purposes.

## Change in Accounting not Operations

Another critical point is that the changing of accounting policies should not change the operations of a company nor of a nonprofit. Hence, if an NPO changes from US GAAP to IFRS, it does not necessitate a change in the reporting to the donor unless the donor requests that change in their reports. This is a very important clarification to make with donors. There may be a push to move to IFRS and this makes sense as many donor countries contribute to a given NPO. Hence, you could have a US donor that would understand that the entity must report in IFRS but for them, their reports may be required to be completed in US GAAP. To achieve this, the accounting systems must be properly set up to be able to accomplish this. The only change that could occur with any transition is a change in how certain transactions are recorded, but not how operations are run. There may be a slight change in how the company records those transactions and may even require a slightly more complex financial reporting system, but the day to day operations should not be affected by the adoption of IFRS.

In a regular company (for-profit) the way these transactions are recorded will affect the way they present their income statement and that may cause a change in the valuation of a company. However, this should rarely occur, any change in reporting standards should not change the financial situation or profitability of any company. Ultimately these changes should result in better comparability and better ways to value companies. In the short run, it may lead to some companies being valued differently, if however, the information is widely known, this should not be a significant factor. The end goal will be better comparisons from US companies and international companies. It is important to note that any change in accounting policies should not result in a change in operations of a company or a nonprofit, nor should it affect the valuation of a company or whether a donor should contribute to a given NPO or not.

### Challenges of IFRS and Nonprofits
When we consider IFRS for nonprofits, it is important to understand that most nonprofits do not have shareholders and most are not valued by profits over time. An investor looks at future expected profits of a company before he or she decides to invest or not. A company that is predicted to make very large sums of profits over the next twenty years will be more highly valued than one with fewer profits. The price/earnings (P/E) ratio is a critical ratio when looking at a stock price, this would be price divided by earnings per share. The higher the P/E ratio, the more likely it is that the company is expecting growth. Hence, if a company earned $8 M profit last year and had one million shares were outstanding, if the price of that stock was $80/share. Then it would have a P/E ratio of 10. The earnings per share would be $8. This is a decent ratio, but this ratio could be much higher if the company is expected to have significant growth over the next few years or many years. If that same company was expected to be earning $80 M profit in five years, this would imply tremendous growth and the stock would have an expected value in five years of approximately $800. Once this growth is known and looked on as reasonable, the share price would now be expected to rise closer to $800, while currently at $80, the immediate effect of this would be a significant rise in

share prices. Fortunately, the information does not come in this fashion all at once. In reality, what does happen is that companies miss their targets or exceed their targets, and this will have a direct effect on share prices, this generally occurs gradually over time.

Nonprofits do not have shareholders and do not trade their shares on the stock exchange. The whole valuation of an NPO is completely different. They are valued intrinsically as how much impact they put out versus how much resources are used. The first part of the equation is extremely difficult to measure accurately and extremely difficult to put a value on. These are two major issues and there are more. The resources being used is much easier to measure, that would be the costs or donor funds that are used during the year. This is a large challenge for IFRS and nonprofits, the very rationale used for IFRS and accounting standards in general make good sense for a company but not as much for a nonprofit.

Comparing two for-profit companies can be quite straight forward and objective. In simple terms, one can measure success through the income statement, are there profits, are they growing, is there an increase in market share? As well, one can look at share prices, has the stock of company A increased more than company B in relative size? These are all strong and objective indicators that one company can be doing better than another.

**Complex Comparisons**
Comparing nonprofits can be far more complex than this, there are no share prices to compare. Although a good proxy for this would be the signing up of new donors or the increase in funding from existing donors, in essence, a larger amount of new donors being signed could be a proxy indicator for success. As there may be fluctuations from year to year, it may be a good idea to compare the past three year trends. Hence, in 2020, you would look at the cumulative total of new contracts signed in 2020, 2019 and 2018. This way the results of one very weak year or

one very strong year will not greatly affect this on the whole, but their effect will be much less so. One may feel that a good way to measure this would be to look at actual spending. This has its merits but also its weaknesses. You may have great funding that was raised two years ago, and that funding is for the next five years, hence, this will show a great increase in spend for five years. It will be less affected by a two or three-year trend of decreased fundraising. Hence, one of the best ways to determine the success of an NPO is its ability to attract new funding and retain current donors. Donors will not fund an NPO that they feel is inefficient, ineffective, lacks trust or is not aligned with their priorities. Hence, the best way to gauge this is newly signed donor funding and not by donor spend.

The donor looks at all the information available to them and decides on several factors, does the NPO have the same priorities, is it trustworthy, efficient and effective. When they see a project that is lined up to their priorities, they look at the NPO and decide whether the most impact will come from giving funds to that NPO. If they feel that their resources do not get as much impact, they will look to other NPOs where more impact can be achieved for the same resources.

### Challenges for Accounting and Nonprofit
Both US GAAP, IFRS, and any GAAP have a real difficulty when it comes to nonprofits, the way a nonprofit is evaluated is completely different from a for-profit company. It will likely take years before something is put together and agreed upon. For now, nonprofits are supposed to follow IFRS but it is understood that IFRS is not fully ready for nonprofits, this is an area that they are working on. The reality is that all GAAPs have been working on this issue for quite some time and so far there has been little progress made.

One needs to look at the intentions of the readers of the financial statements for most companies the intended users are investors and potential investors, while the readers of the financial statements of nonprofits are very different and their intentions are completely different. The main reason that investors look at financial statements is to ensure that they are getting good value for the price they are paying for the stock. This requires reviewing the income statement and balance sheet of the company. The user of the financial statements for nonprofits are not looking for a return on their investment, they are looking at the possibility of getting results for a given contribution. For most standard financial statements this is not even part of the equation. Hence, they are years if not decades away from meeting the needs of the users of the readers of the financial statements for nonprofits.

# CHAPTER 13 - ROLE OF CEO AND CFO

"INTEGRITY IS THE MOST VALUABLE AND RESPECTED QUALITY OF LEADERSHIP. ALWAYS KEEP YOUR WORD." - BRIAN TRACY

The CEO's role is to look after the whole organization this is the same in a for-profit and a nonprofit organization. The CEO should ensure that the organization is moving in the correct direction and is delivering as expected. In a for-profit organization, one simple way to measure whether a CEO is doing well is that they are improving profits. This measurement is not the same in a nonprofit organization and is not as simple to measure. We can look at other ways to measure the performance of a CEO in a nonprofit organization, a similar approach is looking at the funding level of an NPO. One can also look at the overall strength of their reserves to determine this.

**Measuring Success in a Company**

It is far easier to measure success in a for-profit organization, one can simply look at whether they are meeting their quarterly targets or not. One can look at the direction of the CEO and see whether that direction is agreed to and being met. This will affect their profits and ultimately the price of their shares. When shareholders see a sharp decline in their share prices, they will ask for answers and it is usually the CEO and potentially some Board members that are changed when this occurs. This is easy to see with publicly traded companies and relatively easy to do with privately held companies, as well.

In a nonprofit, one must look to other factors, one major factor is the strengthening or weakening of the reserves and the other good indicator would be the total of newly signed agreements compared to prior years. Should a CEO be performing poorly, there are no share prices that can decline and as well there are no shareholders that will request the removal of the CEO and the Board, hence, this is one weakness that many nonprofits currently have. They are not overseen by shareholders who can hold both the Board and the CEO accountable. This is a critical issue that should be considered by donors, if a Board is not acting responsibly, they may answer to no one, leaving donors no where to turn.

### Role of the CFO
The CFO must ensure that financial reporting allows the CEO to make decisions about the future direction that will affect the viability of the company or NPO. The CFO must ensure that the CEO is given the most accurate and relevant financial information on a timely basis.

The CFO must ensure that the internal controls are effective and efficient across the company or NPO. They must work with the external auditors to ensure that they understand and ultimately provide a positive opinion regarding the fairness of the presentation of the financial statements. The CFO must be able to work with the external auditors so that they understand any policies used by the NPO and the reason that they are being used.

They must advise the CEO when certain actions could result in a worsening of profits or sustainability in the case of an NPO. A good CFO will always prepare a cost-benefit analysis of any proposed action and then give their opinion to the CEO. The CFO must ensure that there are reports in place that can quickly inform the CEO whether things are going in the right direction or the wrong direction.

## Joint Responsibility

Ultimately, the primary role of a CEO and CFO is to oversee the profitability of a company while in an NPO it is to oversee the sustainability, in other words, the strength of the reserves and strength of new donor funding trends. These are the two main officers that are directly responsible for the profitability of a company. Others take a major role, but with traditional companies, these are the two major positions that oversee the profitability. It is also why the two positions are paid the highest and they are the two of the most well-known roles in a company. The same is ultimately true for an NPO. However, rather than overseeing profitability they are overseeing sustainability. Sustainability would be the measure of financial health in a nonprofit environment. Ultimately, the CEO is responsible for the results of an NPO. These results will determine if more or less donor funding is given, this in turn, has a direct effect on the sustainability or viability of a nonprofit. The CFO ensures that with whatever level of funding is given to the NPO that the most wise decisions are made to ensure sustainability. Hence, with lower estimates for revenues, the CFO will provide options to the CEO in order to manage the reduced funding. It is up to the CEO to heed the advice of the CFO.

## Role of the CEO vis-a-vis the CFO

The CEO must understand that the CFO is the financial expert and the CEO is the expert on the overall direction and end results of the company. Hence, when a CFO gives information and suggests a direction to the CEO concerning finances, the CEO should, for the most part, take that information and fully understand it. If the CEO rejects the information, he or she should be very aware of what they are doing and be absolutely sure that they are correct.

For the most part, when a CEO disagrees with a CFO it is based on financial information that a CFO presents to that CEO. The

CFO is usually presenting the CEO information of a financial nature, it is the CFO that has the experience and expertise in this area. The CEO generally does not have this same ability. This explains why, for most of their interactions, a CEO will agree with a CFO. Problems are likely to occur when a CEO stops listening to their CFO, especially when the CFO is discussing financial matters.

The CFO is not likely to warn the CEO unless things are not progressing well. If everything is going well financially speaking, the CFO will represent this in their reports and the CEO will be pleased and agree. Generally, when the CFO starts to disagree with the CEO, it is because the direction that the CEO is taking is wrong or it is harming the sustainability of the NPO. It is exactly at this point that a wise CEO will not only listen to their CFO but listen that much more closely. If the CEO resents the CFO for showing them that the financial position is weakening, then this situation quickly goes from bad to worse. This is true in either a for-profit company or a nonprofit.

### Relationship Scenarios
The way the relationship works best between a CEO and a CFO is when both are very qualified. In this case, the CEO will understand that the CFO is qualified and allow them their free reign. This is the ideal situation and this situation covers most of the cases. In most cases, both the CFO and CEO are strong and capable and their relationship will be fully cooperative.

The other situation where the will get along is where both are equally incapable. In this case, it will be a situation where ignorance is bliss. The institution will pay in the long run but these two will likely get along as co-workers. They will get along but this will lead to poor results, neither will understand why the NPO is failing before it may be too late. This is the worst possible scenario, but it is also the least common.

### Difficult Combination
There are two cases where the relationship does not work, this

is when one is talented and the other is not talented. If the CEO is the talented one and the CFO is the less talented one, this is not the end of the world. The CEO will quickly realize the shortcomings of the CFO and either supplement them or replace them. Since the talented one is in the driver seat this can be turned around quickly without causing much damage. As well, since the CEO is the talented one, the company or NPO will be going in the right direction. It will be the CFO wrongly telling the CEO that the company is struggling or making poor decisions. This situation is very rare. There is very little incentive for a weak CFO to tell a strong CEO that they are poorly performing, where they are not. This is an extremely rare situation but one that is possible, just not that plausible. The reality is that the less talented CFO would likely just fully agree with the more talented CEO and the relationship would still work. Even not so talented CFOs can understand when a company or a nonprofit is moving in the right direction with strengthening profitability or sustainability, in the case of nonprofits. Hence, there would be an incentive for the weak CFO to remain silent and likely that is what they would do.

The other situation where this relationship does not work is where the CEO is not very talented or worse is very untalented as a CEO and he has a talented CFO. This situation is more dire. The problem with this situation is that a very untalented CEO will likely be also very insecure since they are not talented. It is this person that makes a lot of mistakes but cannot admit to any errors, there is a fear of them being found out for their inabilities. Hence, rather than admit to making mistakes, there is a constant need to blame others. This person is also very unlikely to listen to a talented CFO. They will be very afraid of sharing the limelight. This person will also want to show their dominance. This is all made worse by both parties knowing that the CEO is not talented and as well that the CFO is talented. This will cause jealousy and resentment from the CEO to the CFO. It will also cause the CEO to not listen to the good advice from the CFO and cause the operations of the organization to falter that much faster. In this situation, there is very little chance of resolving this situation without having the Board step in and force a correction.

In this situation, it is also far more dire as the talented CFO cannot fire the untalented CEO. In short, an untalented CEO is a recipe for a disaster for an organization. In profit organizations, there are far more checks and balances in place to ensure that a person who is not ready or capable does not get handed this role. In nonprofits, these checks and balances are less well-defined and do not prevent the wrong person from attaining these roles. As well targets are far less well-defined in the nonprofit than they are in the company. One can immediately see whether revenues are falling or profits are falling, it is not as easy to determine how much sustainability is being lost without using far more complex indicators in a nonprofit.

### Ideal Reporting line of CFO
Due to the potential problems of a weak CEO overseeing a strong CFO, the CFO should always report directly to the Board and not directly to the CEO. If the CFO reports directly to the CEO, it would be far more difficult for the CFO to disagree with the CEO when they are incorrect. It will also be easier for the CEO to terminate the CFO when the CEO may not appreciate being told that they are incorrect. By correcting the reporting line and ensuring that the CFO does not report directly to the CEO, the nonprofit can be run a lot more smoothly and this will force better cooperation between the two critical roles.

### Role of the Board
The only real answer to a weak and ill-equipped CEO is having a strong Board, which can turn around and resolve these matters. The issue is that really there are some very good Boards out there but there are some less capable Boards as well. If a poorly run board decides to hire a CEO that is not ready for the post and perhaps will never be ready, then that organization is in for a very bumpy ride. The board will likely not have the

strength to realize that the CEO is not talented and should be removed. They will also have the issue of not wanting to admit their mistakes, they hired the CEO in the first place. In this sort of scenario, it is possible to see an organization be completely ruined within a few short years. By the time, the damage is fully known, it will be too late. The issue in this case really comes down to how do you ensure that you have a properly managed board that will make the right decisions. It may be easier for the Board to blame the situation on issues that were out of their control and the control of the CEO than to admit to their own mistakes.

The issue of the board is also further problematic in a non-profit organization, whereas, in a profit organization the board is overseen by the shareholders, hence, if they are not pulling their weight, there can be repercussions and removals. In a non-profit organization, there are no shareholders, hence the board is not responsible or required to report to anyone. It would make sense that as an analogy, the board should report to the major donors in some way, but this is not common. Having this in place in some form or other may be the only chance to save a poorly functioning Board which will result in a failing NPO. It is possible to have a poorly functioning board, that decides to extend their terms. It could even be far worse, where they extend the weak but compliant Board members and get rid of the good but non-compliant board members. There would be no remedy for a situation like this. The board would be reckless and in this case very unlikely to remove themselves from their role. There would be no other way to remove them. The only thing a donor could do would be to decide to not fund them. This is a very hard choice to make, as the organization may have been doing some good work in the past and there may be some current ongoing projects that are necessary to continue. In this case, a donor could be put in a very difficult choice whether to fund or not fund, historically they may appreciate the NPO but currently they may not appreciate the current management team or Board.

This choice faced by the donors would be a tough one, do you knowingly fund an organization that you know is performing poorly with a poorly functioning CEO and Board or do you stop funding them. In the long run, the first option of funding them is just postponing the future and causing an institution to have a long and extended death. As well, if there are some changes made, the damages of a prolonged death would be far more difficult to overcome than a short removal of funding which would cause an immediate reaction.

## How to Fix

An analogy would be a person who has cancer, you have two options one is that you leave it alone and hope for the best and the second one is that you treat it with chemotherapy. The cancer treatment generally is quite poisonous and is akin to killing the cells. The idea here is that to save the person, you must cause damage to that person. In a sense, almost killing the person but then in the process killing the cancer and removing it, once this is accomplished, you can then go on to rebuild the health of the individual. In many cases, if done early enough, the person is fully cured with no signs of cancer. But if left untreated, the cancer will grow and there will be a point that there will be no turning back. There are two main ways to cure cancer, one is to surgically remove it and the other would be to treat the patient with chemotherapy. This is very similar to the situation of a weak CEO, one is removal and the other would be not funding the NPO, this will force the Board to take action, sooner or later, but before major permanent damage can occur.

## Role of Donors

Hence, in a situation like this, the best and most benevolent action of a donor would be to stop any funding and require immediate changes until the situation is rectified. If not, the donor may unwittingly and with all good intentions cause the organization to go bankrupt and without any possibility of revival. It may seem like a strong reaction but where the donors can see that both the Board and the CEO are not acting in the best interests of the NPO, there is no other alternative. To continue funding this NPO would cause the most damage in the long run. Surgical removal would be the case where the board or the shareholders remove the CEO. Most donors do not have this power, hence, the only option to them is reducing funding which hurts both the CEO and the nonprofit. Ultimately, this is better in the long run because not addressing the issue could have far worse consequences down the road. As well, not funding the nonprofit will send a clear message to the Board, which may cause them to make the right correction.

A donor may, understandably, not want to get involved in the management of an organization. While this is a lofty goal and in many cases the right goal. The reality is a donor decides whether to fund or not to fund an organization and that in itself is getting involved in the management of a nonprofit organization. As well, for better governance, they do not need to have daily oversight, but they should get involved when it is clear that some issues are occurring.

The question now becomes what should a donor do, when they understand that a CEO is going in the wrong direction but agree with the overall goals of the nonprofit. They generally do not have any power that would be able to tell the board what to do, as shareholders have in the for-profit companies. This is a big weakness that many donors must face. Without the ability to appoint the board, the donors have no power in this situation and are forced to sit on the sidelines. This is not correct. The donors should not accept this situation. The best-run nonprofits have significant involvement with various donors. It is wise to have an advisory board made up primarily from donors that review the operations of the NPO and that of the Board. They would be able to step in where they feel that something is going wrong. This would give them a direct say in how the Board is acting and how the CEO is acting, as well, the overall direction of the NPO. This should be a standard set up and this is particularly important as the nonprofit does not have any equivalent body as the shareholders.

# CHAPTER 14 - INTERNAL AUDIT FUNCTION

T he internal audit function is critical to both the for-profit entity and nonprofit entity, but there are some differences in how they work and what their goals may be.

The main reason to have an internal audit department is to have an impartial and independent or partially independent assessment of your internal controls. They are there to provide oversight and to help improve efficiency. They can be used to offer advice on how to improve the internal control function or help assess the overall risk to an organization. In some cases, the internal audit function also reviews risk, but in some cases, these functions are separated. When the entity is smaller these two may be combined and when larger they are more likely to be separated.

**Annual Audit versus Internal Audit**
This functions very differently to an annual audit that the company or NPO has every year performed by external auditors. In the case of internal audit, the mandate is very different. The

external auditor may or may not rely on your internal controls, which will depend on their assessment of the effectiveness of your internal controls. The internal auditor will give a review of the overall control environment and provide ways to potentially improve the internal controls. The internal audit team could be requested to look at specific departments or specific functions to determine if some adjustments or improvements are required. The external audit function has one mandate and that is to provide an opinion on the fairness of the presentation of your financial statements.

The advantage of an internal audit is that it is generally outside the operational line from the units that they are auditing. Hence, if an internal audit team is reviewing the finance function, it is ideal that the internal audit team does not report to the CFO or controller, who is responsible for the function. This could pose a conflict of interest and would likely weaken or potentially weaken the results of such an audit.

There are a few aspects that an internal audit team can play a particularly strong role alongside their traditional roles. The internal audit function can review the donor team and ensure that reports are going out as they should. A very critical function would be the review of the M&E team. These are two critical functions in an NPO that are not typically found in a company. As well, the finance team is structurally very different from a for-profit company finance team.

**Team Composition**
The question of who belongs within a given internal audit team is very critical. One key element is that it must be impartial and unbiased. This is where some areas can be tricky and careful thought must be put in to get this done properly. In a large organization, this is not much of an issue, as you can hire dedicated people to achieve this function. Hence, if you have thousands of staff and your budget is over $ 500 M per year, it should

not be an issue to spend an additional $ 500 K a year on this function. As such, you can hire staff where their sole function is internal audit, thus creating an internal audit team. The organization would have to be large enough that there is enough work for them annually and large enough to pay for their salaries and travel. In smaller organizations with a staff of one thousand or less and a budget of $100 M or less, this is not a viable option. It would be very challenging to spend 0.5% of your budget on internal audit and there would not likely be enough work for them to do this full-time. Within a short while, there would also be internal audit fatigue, as the internal audit function may get in the way of operations. Hence, for smaller organizations having a dedicated internal audit team may do more harm than good.

**Balancing Audit Work**

It is important to balance this audit work, you want interaction but you do not want the team to be over-interacting and thus becoming bothersome and interrupting their work. This is a challenge for smaller organizations. There are two main solutions for the smaller sized NPO and each have their pros and cons. The first approach is to outsource this work, find a consultant that can take on this role as an internal auditor on a part-time basis. This has a few advantages since it is a consultant if you are not happy you can move on. In addition, since it is a consultant, you will truly get an independent opinion of the team's work. As well, since you are hiring a consultant, you can find one that specializes in internal audit and has the proper experience and training to carry out these audits. With an external consultant, you would not have any issues with independence.

The other approach is to have your existing staff fulfill this function on a part-time basis. This is also a great approach and one of the more common approaches used. The challenge with this approach is finding a person with the proper skills and who is not part of the team that is being audited, where bias can set in. The best group of individuals to perform this function are usually part of the finance team, as there should be many qualified accountants or other individuals with experience to be able to take on this task very well. The challenge will come when doing an internal audit of the finance team. This may pose an issue, while the person will have the expertise, for the internal audit function to work, the team must be unbiased. Hence, it would be very difficult to audit your own department. This can be achieved if you have two separate finance units or one fiance unit from another region or department, that is not reporting directly to the unit being audited. Again, this would not often occur and tends to only occur with larger nonprofits. Another option, which is not often used but would be a great solution is to have an unrelated but similar organization have a review of your team and you, in turn, would review their team. In the ideal situation, there could be a number of these institutions and where they each share this function among them. There are some challenges with each approach, hence, one simple solution is to have the finance team coordinate all audits and have an external consultant perform the internal audit on the finance team, once every two to three years. This would be the least costly approach and meet all the standards. Hence, one would derive all the benefits but with the lowest costs.

**In-house versus External**
The best strategy, for large organizations, would be to develop an in-house team and provide this function across the organization. The role should be filled with full-time people and from time to time they can pull in some individuals on a part-time basis to assist with a specific internal audit. This would be the gold standard. The advantage here is that the function is truly internal and this allows the team to have a very strong understanding of the business and operations, it will reduce the amount of lead time, as they do not have to learn about the business each time they perform an audit. As well, since they

are a separate team they are completely unbiased as they would be auditing other units or departments. One may ask, who will audit the internal audit function, the answer is simple, you could have the finance team audit the internal audit function. This approach can only be efficient if the organization is sufficiently large.

For smaller entities that cannot afford to hire a completely separate team, the best and most efficient approach is for the internal audit function to be handled on a part-time basis from the finance team. This way you will ensure that the proper expertise exists for executing and managing the internal audit function. This will work for all units that are not reporting to the finance team, for those units and the finance team itself an internal audit should be performed by an external consultant or by a similar institution that has agreed to perform this function. A second approach would be to outsource the whole function but this would be more costly and have some inefficient components, hence an approach that combines the two is the most cost-effective alternative.

### Reporting Line of Internal Audit Function

The reporting line of an internal audit team is critical. Often these teams report to the CEO or the CFO and this is not an optimal solution, as the concept of impartiality is broken. The CEO and CFO will have many units reporting to them and hence, if the internal auditor also reports to one of these two, there could be an issue with impartiality. It is important to note, that just the fact that the internal audit function has a common reporting line, does not mean that they will not act independently, but the chance that this would occur is much more likely. It is very difficult to review the unit you supervise and it is very difficult to tell your boss that something they are doing is not working optimally. Some people can do this and some bosses appreciate that honesty, unfortunately for every one that appreciates that honesty, there are many that do not.

It is interesting that the people who tend to appreciate honest feedback are the ones that are generally doing quite well. Hence, the constructive criticism is less required and those that are underperforming and desperately require feedback that may be critical or constructive are the ones least likely to be willing to accept that feedback. These individuals are poor leaders and can even retaliate against a person that says something negative. Hence, when you are going to give poor feedback to your boss or constructive criticism to your boss, it is important to know, if your boss overall is a solid achiever or a poor achiever. If they are in the former group then go ahead and be honest, if they are in the second group, still, be honest but very careful and start looking for a new boss that you can look up to.

## Should not report to CFO or CEO

If the CFO and the CEO is not the best person for the internal audit team to report to, then who is? The internal audit team should report independently and should report to the board or a board member who has been appointed or voted to cover this function. It is important to choose a board member that has some experience in finance or accounting. It can be done with a layperson, but there could be a steep learning curve and this would not help the overall audit function. This board member will likely have to sometimes choose between the internal auditor's findings and what the CFO or CEO may say, should there be a difference of opinion. Hence, giving this role to just any board member is not a great idea, it should be one that has some knowledge of this function and is completely independent of the CEO. The board member chosen to lead the internal audit function must have some expertise with the subject matter.

There may be a case, where the internal auditor disagrees with something the CEO is doing. In most cases, this can be resolved between the internal auditor and the CEO, but in some cases, if the situation is so critical, the CEO may not want to budge on his position, if the internal auditor also does not want to budge, then the main way this is handled is that the internal auditor will write it up in their report as a major issue. The management response will say it is a non-issue and give their reasons why. If the situation is so dire and verges on fraud or corruption, then the internal auditor must bring it up to the board and the board should make any necessary changes. It may mean looking at the situation from another viewpoint or the board reviewing the matter directly.

This is only a role that can be undertaken by an internal auditor that does not report to management. It would be very hard for that same individual to be completely honest with his or her boss, knowing that his reviews would be very much negatively affected. The good internal auditor will stick with his principles but many decent internal auditors will bend under this pressure. Hence, the reporting lines are very important and the internal auditor should not fear any repercussions from their honesty. The only way to achieve this is by having the internal audit team report directly to the board.

## Critical Principle of Success
A strong internal audit function is critical to ensure that risks are being addressed and that the company and its departments are working efficiently. If this role is not taken seriously there could be some serious consequences to the organization or the company.

# CHAPTER 15 -
# STRATEGY FOR
# NONPROFITS

"A VISION WITHOUT A STRATEGY REMAINS AN ILLUSION." - LEE
BOLMAN

T he nonprofit must have a coherent strategy that can be viewed by donors to see where the goals and priorities of the nonprofit are and how they expect to achieve them. The strategy should be set by management and agreed to by the Board.

## Strategy and Fundraising

This strategy can be crucial with regards to fundraising. If done right, it should ensure that the current donors are pleased with the strategy and are in agreement with it, ideally, the donors would have had some input into its development. The highly functioning and effective nonprofit, not only consider their donors but more importantly asks for their specific input. The worse thing that can occur is that a nonprofit creates a new strategy where they did not consult their current major donors and the donors disagree with the strategy. This would result in very poor consequences, and for this reason, an NPO should always consult with its key donors before approval and even before starting the strategy. The second worse result would be not consulting the donors and they agree with the essence of your new strategy. The best result is consulting with them and having them in line with your strategy and also having a say in that strategy. Hence, the only way one achieves the best result is by having the donors play a part in the creation of the strategy. Equally important is to have the intended beneficiaries of your work also play as an integral partner in this process. If you are looking to help the poor, you need to be able to reach out to these communities and get input on how to best help them. All the key partners to the nonprofit must be included in this process, from donors, to key stakeholders and beneficiaries.

A nonprofit that feels they can do it alone without donor input will tend to push away donors and this will lose support. Do not make a mistake of not including your major partners and donors into the process of creating your strategy. This is a clear recipe for failure, both for the strategy and for the nonprofit.

The more eyes on a strategy the better the results or outcome. By not, including your major partners in the process, you are creating two major issues. You are not keeping them in the loop and you are not hearing the invaluable feedback from these critical partners. You are likely to have a worse outcome. Additionally, you will garner less support from your partners, you will also have a worse strategy, and as a result, you will be off to a horrible start and may never recover from this, until your next strategy and hopefully prepared with a different team that does know how to reach out to its critical partners.

### A Solid Strategy

A strategy is not a very complex matter. What you need to start with is what issues is the nonprofit trying to resolve. Are you working on poverty? Are you working on hunger? Are you working on education? Medical access? AIDS? There are a host of challenges that the world faces and a lot of good that can be done by nonprofits. Once you can state what your objective is within a few sentences. You need to think about which populations of people that you are aiming to help. If you are working on ridding the world of poverty, where are your intended beneficiaries? Are you looking to work primarily in Africa, primarily in Asia or world-wide? This must also be clarified. This should be accomplished very quickly with a nonprofit that knows who they are and what they do and for whom. In essence, all NPOs must know this immediately and intrinsically.

You then need to think about the next five to ten years. What are your expected outcomes for the next five years? What are they for the next ten years? During this step, it is necessary to consider contribution levels and expected outcomes. To do this correctly, a minimum of four main units must work closely together. You need the strategy department, management (CEO), finance unit and M&E department to work closely together. To start with you would need to look at likely funding levels over the next five to ten years, this can be done by the donor team and finance. A good estimate is critical to starting your plan. Then you need to agree on the lowest estimate level, the likely level, and a reasonable optimal level.

If your likely level is $100 M per year, then over the next five years you will have funding of $500 M, you could have a low estimate at 60% this would be $300 M and a optimistic level at 40% higher or at $700 M. The next step would be to estimate the future outcomes, results, and impacts with this funding. This will not be easy, but it is necessary to get this right. This is where the M&E team will need to get to work and estimate future outcomes. They should be believable based on past results and logical. There should be a balance between being aspirational but also reasonable. They should also involve a range for each level of funding.

For each funding level, one should have a range of expected outputs, outcomes, and the impact that one can summarize and present within the strategy. Ideally, it would also follow with the United Nations Sustainable Development Goals (SDGs). There are 17 of these SDG's and you should have overlap to as many of these goals as possible, and be able to demonstrate how much you can contribute to these goals

## Why are these steps important to create a coherent strategy?

If you cannot reasonably show the impact that a donor's contribution will have and especially concerning the UN - SDG's, you will have a hard time to market your value proposition. Platitudes will not sell to the donor class, results and expected results will. You need to be able to demonstrate a history of results and that you have made reasonable efforts to estimate, what your results are or will be. This will go a long way to get further acceptance with the donors.

### The Strategic Plan

The next critical element will be the plan. It is a step forward to having the expected results over the next coming number of years, but how will that be achieved is critical as well. Will you be opening new areas of business? Will you be scaling up certain projects? Will there be new partnerships that must be created or strengthened to achieve these results? A plan would be critical to driving the reasonableness of the results estimated. How many projects will need to be running? Will you need completely new projects or the current mixture or projects that you already have? Which project areas will you focus on and which regions? Are you saying that you will lower poverty in a given country, but have no operations in that country currently? What is your plan to get your results there? Will you open an office? Will you work remotely? Will you hire some consultants to achieve this? It is important, that for the vast majority of the impact you state that you will achieve, that there is a reasonable plan to do so. If there is no reasonable explanation for your expected impact, then you will lose credibility and your funding will drop. It is critical that these steps are performed and that the impact is reasonable.

## Value for Money

The concept of value for money is critical in nonprofit and the value that a nonprofit can deliver are: its outcomes and impact, hence, there must be a positive relationship between those two. The value is not stated in dollar terms, but there is an implied value to many of these outputs, even if they are hard to define or not reliably measurable. When any donor reviews a project of an NPO. The first thing that they will consider is what return there is on the investment or what impact will this project have. If they invest $1 M, they are expecting to have outcomes and impact with a value of at least $1 M, if another entity can deliver the same results for $0.5 M, then why should they pay another entity twice the cost. An important caveat here is the reliability of results, if both entities have the same history of delivering results, then it would be very likely that a given donor would fund the project with the same or similar results for half the cost.

One needs to have a good idea of what is a reasonable cost for a given outcome or impact, then ensure your costs are in line with this. If a project cannot get results or impact that is of higher perceived value than the costs to achieve those impacts, it is not an efficient or effective project. This level of efficiency with projects is a critical principle to success. A nonprofit that can deliver strong results with low costs is a big step closer to success. If a nonprofit cannot deliver strong results at a reasonable costs, then success will be severely limited. If a project within an entity cannot become efficient, then that project will not be funded, for the most part, and that project will not be workable by that nonprofit. Entities must look for projects and work where they are competitive or can soon become competitive. Sometimes the entity should stick with projects where they are competitive or where they hold a competitive advantage.

This is not always so clear, as many organizations may have a lot of unrestricted funding or have direct and significant funding by a closely related government or entity. This fact alone may grant a competitive advantage to an entity. Hence, an entity can, in essence, subsidize their work on a given project. On individual projects, this may be a factor, but on the overall effectiveness of an institution, it may have the opposite effect. In other words, other funds can pay to do the work for that project, thus making it look more efficient, but this cannot be achieved when looking at the entire NPO as a whole. An entity that has a large supply of funding that is completely unrestricted, may tend to be less efficient and have more waste. Steps should be taken not to go down this road, as a donor should not only look at a given project but should also look at the entire results and compare that to the same funding level. In some cases, organizations with a large source of earned funding or unrestricted funding can end up being less efficient and may not need to charge full-costs to donors. This poses an issue, as donors may prefer to fund the projects with an overall lower price tag, but this may be hurting those nonprofits that may be more effective and efficient but have less earned income or unrestricted funds to supplement projects. There is no easy answer with this one, but all donors should consider the overall effectiveness of an NPO and not just the price put on a project for a given amount of outcome and impact.

To illustrate this, let us take two NPO's X and Y. Let us say that X has no unrestricted funding and has a funding level of $80 M per year and Y has the same funding but also $20 M in unrestricted funding. Let us say that it uses $10 of that unrestricted funding to subsidize their $80 M, and let us assume that they will now deliver 5% more due to that subsidy. Hence, their outputs and outcomes are 5% higher, but with the additional $10 M they are going to hire larger support teams and produce very little additional results. When comparing on a project to project basis, any donor will look at the two projects and state that a project in NPO Y is more efficient as it delivers 5% more for the same cost. Hence, they are more likely to fund those projects, but in reality, the NPO X is more efficient because it is delivering 95% of the results for an overall 80% of the overall costs.

## Efficiency of a Nonprofit

Hence, a donor should consider not only the efficiency of the project but also the overall efficiency of the organization. This may happen to some extent but for the most part, most donors likely look at two main factors, the reliability of the NPO and the expected value to be delivered or the output and outcomes that are expected versus the costs to achieve these outcomes and impacts. This approach may tend to favor nonprofits that have a competitive advantage such as earned income or high levels of unrestricted funding. While there is no easy resolution to this issue, it is something that should be considered, as well.

Ideally, it would be good if we were able to compare the project's outputs, outcomes, and impacts while taking out the subsidy in a project or at a minimum including the subsidy in the grant. Hence, the true value for money can be evaluated.

## A Necessary Tool

In summary, a strategy is a necessary tool for any nonprofit organization to not only attract funding but also give it a guide of where the organization should go. It can allow an organization to measure itself against expected outcomes and impacts, as time passes. A good strategy will also lend credence to an entity and explain to an outside reader, what they are trying to achieve. The strategy should be reviewed every year to make sure that they are on target or whether they are falling behind. If they are falling behind, are there certain circumstances that can explain this lag in performance? If yes, and these are reasonable then the lagging result can be explained and should be. Any lack of explanation of poor performance will lessen the credibility of the strategy as a whole. Hence, there should be a plan to cover any potential lagging results. If this situation is caused by a reduced funding level and those lowered results are reasonable relative to the lowered funding level, then that would be a good explanation. If, however, there is a decreased level of funding by 10% and the outcomes and impact are decreased by 45%, then the funding shortfall cannot, alone, explain the difference and other reasons should be investigated to understand the shortfall in performance. There should be complete transparency with donors and partners for any poor performance of expected results.

In short, a proper strategy is fundamental and it requires a strong strategy unit, a strong management team, a strong M&E team, a strong donor team and significant input from both critical partners, donors, beneficiaries and more. This will have a significant impact on the success or failure of an NPO. The strategy should not be taken lightly and as well should be treated as a living document, which needs to be compared frequently with actual results. By doing this correctly, the NPO is in a good position to start to deliver on that strategy.

# CHAPTER 16 - GOOD GOVERNANCE

**P**roper governance in an NPO is a very important matter, while it is an important matter for all for-profit companies it plays a critical role in an NPO.

In a for-profit environment, it is easier to determine success, are sales going up, are your costs going down. Is your overall market share increasing? Are profits on the rise or falling? These factors are relatively simple to measure and very objective, hence, conclusions can be made very quickly whether a company is on track or not. Whether it is meeting their objectives or not.

## Measuring Results

With a nonprofit, measurement of the results takes a lot longer. Over a long period, one can tell if an NPO is on the right track or it is not. Hence, over five years, it is easy to tell whether an NPO is meeting its objectives or not, but it would be very hard to measure success over a few months. If we take a company that sells smartphones, we can look at the past few months of sales and compare it to previous periods and to estimates to determine the success or failure of operations. This is true because there are millions of very small transactions and hence, positive changes will be very evident very quickly. With an NPO, the fact is that donor agreements are signed only a small number of times throughout the year.

Imagine an NPO with a size of $100 M spend per year, let us say the average grant outstanding is $10 M and the average grant duration is four years. This will mean that the average size grant per year is $2.5 M, and hence there would be roughly 40 grants outstanding every year. It would mean that roughly ten of those grants expire each year, and hence, ten are signed each year. This would be less than one grant being signed every month. The signing of grants also is not evenly spread out, you may have a period where three or four grants are signed in one month and then go months without signing another. Hence, it is not uncommon to go a couple of months, without signing a new grant, in the given example. For NPOs with hundreds of grants signed per year, the average number of grants signed in a month will be far greater.

## Proxy for Determining Success

Since the NPO's ability to sign new grants, can be a good proxy for determining success, this is greatly limited because it would take a long time to see whether the situation is moving poorly or moving in the right direction. Hence, by waiting for results with this, it may be too late. If the first six months there is a sign of a decrease, then management waits for another six months to determine that something is going on, well now a year has passed and the NPO now understands there is an issue but does not know what the issue is nor how to fix it. The NPO might realize they are in trouble but may fear to take any drastic action which could exacerbate the problem. In an FPO, the issue is seen right away due to a strong decline in sales. They can then look at what is the cause of this. Is their product inferior? Is there something wrong with their marketing? A new competitor? This information would be immediately available and the cause would become known, this issue would be quickly addressed and corrected. This is an area that works far better in the for-profit environment as compared to the nonprofit environment.

An increase in donor revenue or a decrease in donor revenue is a great indicator that there is something that donors either appreciate or do not appreciate, but the disadvantage with this indicator is that it is not timely. Once, you figure out that there is an issue it may be too late to take corrective measures. Seeing a steady decline in new donor revenue is the most effective and quickest way to assess a problem.

It is important to build systems across your major functions to be able to determine if they are functioning or not and have reports that tell you this on a monthly or quarterly basis. Creating key performance indicators across units is critical for management to highlight potential issues before they become problematic.

**Budgets and Forecasts**
A critical function in ensuring that the spending is going according to expectations is to develop a strong budget system and forecasting system. Budgets should be prepared and approved before the start of the fiscal year for every part of the organization.

A good budget process will include all relevant parties to that function and be overseen and consolidated by the finance unit. The Project Leader is critical to determining the budget for the year, they will know whether the project will be expanding, hiring or letting go of some staff. These expectations should all be added to prepare the budget. The budget should then be reviewed by the finance team and then finally approved by the project manager. An important role that finance will play is to look at the estimates and see that they are reasonable, achievable, and measurable. The finance team ensures the integrity of the budget process for overall reasonableness, completeness, and accuracy.

Once, the budget is complete and consolidated for the whole organization, it should be approved by both the CEO and the

Board. This should be done prior to starting the year. Hence a budget for fiscal year 2021, must be approved towards the end of fiscal year 2020.

The next steps are to prepare the reports and include estimates for forecasts as the fiscal year begins. The forecast is a critical step and often oversimplified. It is most common for forecasts to be a calculation where the current expenses are simply prorated over the year. This is a very simple approach but one where it adds very little value. It is very simple for any system to prepare a budget to date and then compare it to the spend to date, which is a critical step. However, this step cannot function alone. A good forecasting system can alert you to problems that are not being addressed. Weaknesses here can lead to disastrous results and commonly this process is not given the time and resources that it requires.

As an example, consider a $12 M project for one year, that would be expected to spend about $1 M a month, but let us say that in the tenth month, the project leader knows that there will be a large expense of $5 M. Imagine that project is spending at $1 M per month for the first nine months. A simple look at this project and one will prorate the $9 M cost over 12 months and see that the expected expense over the year would be $12 M. Hence, the reports will show that this project is spending on target. Now the tenth month occurs and immediately there is the average monthly spend of $ 1 M plus an additional cost of $5 M and now the total spend on the project is $15 M, they have already exceeded their budget for the year and two months remain. This sort of situation can lead to a very negative outcome for the nonprofit. The NPO has overspent on a restricted grant and these costs will need to be covered either by other grants or covered by unrestricted funding or worse by the nonprofits reserves.

In this same case, with a forecast system in place, by the end of the first month, it will already be seen that there is a likely going to be an overspend for the year if the monthly costs are not reduced significantly. This is why a strong forecasting system is required. This example highlights a very obvious situation, but there are many situations like this one that are not as obvious, but still result in negative outcomes.

Hence, for good governance, you need a strong functioning finance team and a very strong budget, forecast and reporting function.

## Donor Reporting

A strong donor reporting function is critical. It is important that the donors' reporting needs are met and this team plays a critical role in coordinating that function. This team also plays a key role in coordinating the grant proposal process and delivering them to the donors. This team must coordinate with the project team, the finance team, the M&E team, the strategy team and work with the CEO.

With the finance team, there should be an expected volume of grants signed over a given period, any period missing these targets should be evaluated, and it should be agreed on when the lowering volume of grants being signed is a temporary issue or a trend. A temporary decline could occur for political reasons or world issues that are out of the control of management. There are times when the trend downwards or upwards is because of geopolitical reasons and also there are times when this is occurring due to management issues. One way to understand this, is the two main reasons for a trend whether good or bad would be external issues or internal issues. If the donor funding is declining, the reports should be quickly alerted to that. It is necessary for any NPO with good governance that there are immediate warnings when funding decreases. As well, it is important that if the decrease is in one month, this can be a temporary issue and the balance can be made up in subsequent months. However, when the targets are missed regularly, then after three to six months there should be some alarm bells set off and a clear justification for this decline should be sought. There should be some attempt to determine if the cause is external or internal and whether the cause is likely a short term issue or a long term issue. If the cause is internal, then it is necessary to find the root of the cause and correct the issues immediately. Internal causes are usually a result of management and generally linked to decisions made by the CEO and Board.

This decline should also be factored into the forecast to see the likely effects for this year and years to come. If the decline is permanent and there are not enough reserves to get them through this decline, then it is likely that the NPO will need to cut some costs. This can be a dramatic change. If on average your fundraising was bringing in about $100 M per year, and then it is now getting reduced to about $50 M per year, it is necessary to put a plan in place to reduce your annual spending from $100 M to $50 M. The plan does not have to go into effect immediately as most grants are valid for three to four years, hence, you would be able to make this transition over a three to four year period, but there should be a reasonable plan to get there. While it is important to create this plan, it is even more critical to understand the cause of this decline.

As such, it is critical to know what is going on with fundraising and react swiftly to any shortfalls in projections. One should understand if a shortfall is a temporary one, and caused by an external factor such as a geopolitical event or one that is caused by internal factors such as the overall direction the organization is heading. Once an understanding of the cause is known, then an appropriate remedy should be selected.

### Internal Audit and Risk Function

It is critical to have a strong internal audit and risk function so that any issues that are developing can be found on a timely basis. As well, it is important to look at risks that the NPO may be facing. Is the economy heading into a recession, how will this affect donor contributions? Perhaps a president will be changed in your host country or a very important donor country? Could this have negative consequences? If so, how can they be mitigated?

Looking at the potential risks you face each year is a critical step to ensure that these risks do not materialize and should they become a reality, there should exist a plan to mitigate these risks. Is there sufficient reserves to cover a global recession? If not, are there some other precautions that can be taken?

Without understanding your known risks and evaluating potential risks the NPO will be subject to further risks and might find themselves in a difficult situation without a plan to recover.

The internal audit function will help to ensure that the controls are in place and each unit is doing what they are expected to achieve. This is a critical function and for it to be functioning properly the team should report directly to the Board.

The internal audit and risk assessment functions are critical for an NPO to have good governance.

### Donors and Partners

It is necessary to cultivate constructive relationships with most donors and especially key donors, key stakeholders, and key partners. It is this group that will be best able to assess whether you are heading in a proper direction or perhaps heading in the wrong direction.

At the end of the day, a donor may agree with your direction or disagree with the direction the NPO is heading. If they agree, then they are that much more likely to fund and when they are not in agreement they are that much more likely to not give further funding. It is clear that one cannot please all the people all the time, hence, when a change is made, you may lose one or two donors, but the hope is that in the process you gain one or two, or perhaps even three. Hence, the net effect is neutral or positive. When your overall funding increases, one can say that the donors are in agreement with your direction and when it drops they are not pleased with your direction. If a donor does not see tangible results with a project, they may pull out of that project, but fund another project. This would be the case of losing funding for a given project but not losing the donor overall. If this happens for several projects, then there is a time where it is necessary to evaluate what is going on. Why are these projects failing? If a nonprofit cannot answer this, then it will be struggling.

### Stong engagement with donors should be pursued.

If you have a strong donor engagement process, where the donors are regularly invited to board meetings or specialized donor meetings. This would be a great environment for a donor to raise any concerns. This process should not be led by the donor team, although they may send all the invites and coordinate the activities. The main person who should be responsible for this function would be the CEO of the NPO or the Head of the NPO. When relations are developed very well, the donor can give their input into whether they approve of a given strategy or not. It may seem as though one is taking control away from the organization and giving some to the donors, it is important to remember that the donors are partners to these operations. The bulk of the money being spent is contributed to the NPO by them. They should have some say and that say should be somewhat significant. It is clear, that they already have a strong input because they can choose which projects they appreciate or do not. This will affect the direction that the NPO takes. This effect is very different where the nonprofit can generate their own funds or has one major donor such as, the government of where they reside. In these rare cases, the NPO can have a more direct role in choosing their overall direction. In the end, the success of the NPO, in these rare situations, where the nonprofit does not rely on donor funding, is not based on fundraising, but rather based on their impact alone and being able to maintain their sustainability. It is important to note, that very few nonprofits are in this position, most nonprofits rely heavily on donor funding and hence success can be directly linked to the success of donor fundingraising, which ultimately is also linked to achieving results. Hence, ultimately the success is based on results, which then will lead to increased donor funding, a lack of results will have the opposite effect.

For most nonprofits, it is important to develop strong relations not only to assist with funding but to provide feedback whether they agree with the direction of the institution or the strategy that may have recently been adopted. Without this function, an NPO may be sailing their ship without any navigational devices or sailing blindly. The partnership between an NPO and its donors is critical to success. The donors can give great insight into whether the direction the organization is taking is one that they are comfortable with, agree with, or disagree with. It is also critical to get input from key stakeholders, key partners and beneficiaries for any new strategy that an NPO may be undertaking.

## Donors and Oversight

Another potential role for donors to play is the role of oversight to the board, which is not that common, but if one were to compare it to a for-profit company, one would see that the shareholders appoint the board and hence, can remove members as well. As such, it may make sense that a key group of donors take on this role. A key role would be the appointment of new board members and the removal of ones that are not acting to the expectations set by the donors. Without this role, the Board is not being overseen by anyone and this is not good governance. This may be one of the weakest points of general good governance for a nonprofit, there is generally no oversight of the board at all. They generally report to no one but themselves. This is a key weakness with many NPOs, instituting a Donor oversight Board that has real power in appointing and removing Board members may be a simple correction that could improve good governance significantly. The donors in a sense can play the role of proxy shareholders, by appointing or removing Board members, each major donor which can be defined by the key donors will get a vote. The donors can agree whether it is important to meet or not meet. Hence, when an NPO is running smoothly, it may make sense not to meet, but when running into issues, it may make sense to meet.

## Board of Directors

The Board plays a critical role in governance, they are there to ensure that the management of the NPO is working and that the overall reputation of the NPO is intact.

When a nonprofit starts to lose its direction, the operations can quickly fall apart. The Board has a critical role to play in determining what is the reason for this failure and the best way to correct it. If an NPO has a history of losses, the Board must get in there to correct the situation. The first thing that must be done is the board must speak with the CEO and see if there is a way to correct the issues. The board should also consult with the CFO, separately. For the most part, when a successful NPO starts to fall apart and the only major change has been a change in CEOs, it is often that the problem lies with the new CEO. A CEO that is not ready to take on this role but acts in such a way that indicates he is, would be the worse recipe for the nonprofit. This person will not likely listen to good advice and will do their own thing. When things go awry they will look for anyone to blame. The main role of a Board is to prevent such individuals from leading a nonprofit to failure. A Board should be able to determine when they are dealing with such an individual and the only response is to remove the CEO. Sometimes, it is the board that has chosen this CEO and that may cloud their judgment.

If this situation is allowed to linger for years, it could cause permanent reputational damages and will leave the NPO in a situation where their reserves will have been used up with little to no future benefit and very little prospects. Once a CEO has been removed, it will take a new CEO months, if not a year, to get things back on track. This may be too little too late, especially if the reserves have been severely depleted.

If the Board fails to remove a CEO on a timely basis, they are just as much at fault for the failure of the NPO, as the CEO. If this is the case, it is very likely that the Board should also be replaced, however, without shareholders, the Board often oversees themselves. This is very poor governance.

When everything is working fine, more or less, the role of the Board is there to give feedback and advice on strategy and direction. The main role of a Board would be to oversee management and to take swift decisions when needed. In a sense, when management is doing a great job, the role of the Board is minimal. In the situation of a well-running management team, it will have little effect if the Board is effective or ineffective. However, when management is not acting as they should, this is when you need an effective board. The difference between an effective Board and an ineffective board, is an ineffective Board with a weak CEO will spell ruin for an NPO. A weak CEO with a strong Board will simply result in the board getting rid of the CEO who is not doing their job properly. This simple difference could be the difference from an NPO that is doomed to failure and one that may thrive in a year or two.

In short, a strong Board can rectify a weak CEO but a weak Board will not fix that situation, hence, a weak Board is a very big risk for an NPO and not having any oversight of a Board is another great risk for an NPO. Having a weak Board is similar to not having a secondary parachute, if the primary parachute fails, your survival depends on that secondary chute working.

### Metrics and Evaluation (M&E)

The M&E team plays a critical role in evaluating the success of projects or lack of success. This function is often overlooked but it is a critical function. At the end of the day, the delivery of project results or impact is what an NPO is selling. It is critical to know which projects are working well and which ones are not.

The M&E team can play a pivotal role in this process. Each project has a list of output, outcomes and impact, the M&E team should be the ones to measure this and they should do this scientifically, as much as possible and independently. Another area many nonprofits need to improve is that they put the project team in charge of collecting and reporting the M&E results.

The problem with this is that a project leader will often be biased and want to show the best results to their donors. If these results are not a valid reflection of the true delivery of results, this may cause more harm than good. If a donor loses trust in the M&E reports that you deliver, this is likely caused by exaggerating the results. This can happen with overzealous project leaders and is a good reason why this function should be overseen by a separate unit and not overseen by the person who is leading the project.

If this function is done properly, it will be able to assess which projects are working and which are not. Then, work can go into those projects that are not delivering to find out why this is the case. This is an important step and one that all donors do, to decide which projects to fund. If a donor no longer believes in your results or your M&E reports. It will harm your fundraising. If a project has poor results, the best strategy is, to be honest about the poor results and come up with a plan to improve those results. This will go a long way with the donors, as you are being upfront with some issues before the donor has to ask the questions to you. Trying to hide your poor results through M&E is a very bad strategy. You may fool one donor, but once they figure it out, you will likely never sign an agreement with that donor again.

Every quarter or at a minimum every six months, each project should be reviewed for effectiveness and given a rating, from strong to weak. The ones with strong ratings can continue as they are, these are the ones achieving results, the ones with weak ratings must justify why they are not achieving the expected results and what they will do to correct this. A nonprofit that does not do this is bound to make some errors, it will not know what is a good project and what is a poor project. They will be able to see highly successful projects and great failures but there will be less distinction made between these extremes.

If the general average of your projects are declining in terms of performance, this is important to know and to find out why.

Without a strong M&E function you will not know this until it is too late. The importance of this function still needs to be better understood. Some nonprofits are doing very well with their M&E function and some still have a long way to go, but for the most part, each NPO can improve this function. It is interesting to note that this function is not really necessary in a for-profit environment. The ability to determine profitability is mostly sufficient.

## Chief Executive Officer
The role of the chief executive officer plays a critical role in the success and governance of the NPO. This role should be undertaken by someone who completely understands the business and understands the nonprofit environment. The success of this role is to bring talent together and to drive them to a common goal. The successful CEO must drive better results for projects and this will lead to better results in fundraising.

Whenever a new CEO is brought in there is a period where the donors are getting to know this individual. Generally, there is a honeymoon period, where the person is given the benefit of the doubt and they can do no wrong. This period lasts for three months and up to six or nine months. A new CEO must use this period wisely to form solid relations with key donors. If this is not done within the first six months or so, it will be much more difficult later. Hence a critical strength of this individual is that they can speak with donors and have a positive effect on them. If a CEO cannot achieve this, then they are going to have a very difficult time fulfilling their role. A CEO who cannot achieve this, may blame the donor and say something, like, they just don't like me. This is shifting the blame away from them and on to the donors. The successful CEO will have a positive effect on the results of the nonprofits projects. In essence, the strong CEO must be able to deliver more with the same level of projects or at least maintain. The CEO should explain to the donors as to how they will achieve this. If this cannot be reasonably explained or worse if the donors do not feel the CEO will be able to maintain results, then the results will be problematic. The reality is that if donors are being turned away from a new CEO, it is usually the fault of the CEO, especially if the decline is significant and sustained over a long period. Donors are looking at results and looking to see who they can trust to deliver results, personalities play very little role with donors.

## CEO and Delegation

A good CEO must be able to delegate well, often a strong project person may be promoted to a CEO over a short time. This may work, but oftentimes this individual is a detailed oriented person and to do this new role properly, you must become a big picture person very quickly otherwise, you are sure to fail. The reality is that detailed oriented people cannot generally magically switch to being a big picture person. Many people that have had their roles switched wherein one role they were detailed oriented and now must become big picture people, never actually achieve this transition and are often plagued with the same criticism. Often, they recognize their issue but still are not able to rectify it. It would be like taking someone who excels at hockey and now assume that they must also be good at basketball. People that have always been big picture people can get into the details for a short period of time, but they cannot live in that environment, they cannot do a job that requires detailed work eight hours a day, each day of the year. While, on the other hand, detailed oriented people, have the same problem, they can for short periods of time become big picture people and they can learn this talent, but doing a job full time will be like a fish out of water.

They must be able to delegate well and they must be able to gauge whether a person knows what they are doing or does not. If that person cannot do both of these, they will have a hard time adjusting to the new role and the NPO will suffer until these skills are learned. The truth of the matter is that with some people who have devoted their lives to being a highly detailed orientated person, the shift to becoming a big-picture person is too much and they can never fully make this transition. These CEO's will tend to micromanage strong staff, which will cause resentment. Under this environment, the stronger staff are much more likely to leave and the weaker staff to be promoted. This leaves a much weaker entity. If a CEO has been known to be a highly detail-oriented person, it is not to say they cannot change, but best to see that they can change before promoting them to the CEO.

The right person being hired for this role will have a positive effect on donors and the teams within the organization. This person will know how to motivate teams and will understand that being a micro-manager is completely ineffective, as such, they will delegate a lot, as should be done. This will motivate the teams and the general work and environment will improve. The right person will also be able to gauge good talent and poor talent. He will delegate to those that are strong and look to work closely with the less talented staff.

The right type of person taking on this role can lead to a lot of good, both operationally and from the donor perspective. This will lead to increase funding and will lead to more sustainability for the nonprofit. As well better results will follow. On the other hand, if the wrong person is hired, this will lead to poorer results, good staff leaving, and a loss from donor confidence and donor funding, this, in turn, will cause a loss in the financial strength of a nonprofit and ultimately can cause its demise.

The only way to correct the wrong CEO being hired is having good KPI's from the Board and the Board understanding when they have chosen the wrong individual and correcting the issue promptly.

## Donor Advisory Board

A donor advisory board should be set up that is controlled and run by the top major donors. This board should oversee the board and be given certain rights to terminate board members or not extend board members. There should be a valid reason as to why. This board should review the actions of the Board and write a summary on whether they approve of the direction of the board. This board would need to have the ability to effect changes and act when needed. They could have the ability to approve or disapprove new board members and any extensions. This is critical to good governance otherwise no one is overseeing the board and a poor board will not correct itself. In a for-profit company the non-executive board members are elected by the shareholders, however, most nonprofits do not have shareholders, hence, this group does not exist. What happens is generally the board decides on its own, who the board members are, and who stays and who goes. This occurs with little to no oversight and can be a significant weakness to the nonprofit.

Without a donor advisory board, there is no way to get rid of an incompetent board, the only way is that the incompetent board removes themselves, which is very unlikely. In a situation where they are underperforming, they would prefer to correct it before handing it over, this is where a bad situation turns worse.

This is a major weakness with most nonprofits and most nonprofits would fall into this category of not having a donor advisory board that can take action.

Donors should request that all nonprofits have this in place, otherwise too much power is given to one group and there exists no way to remove that power from that group. All works well when you have an honest and competent board, but things fall apart when an incompetent board comes in. The unfortunate truth is that a competent board is more likely to remove some of its members than an incompetent board, particularly those in more prominent roles, such as the Chair.

# CHAPTER 17
# - RESERVES &
# THEIR ROLE

Reserves are critical for the long term survival of any nonprofit. This ensures strong viability going forward. Hence, in any given year if there is a deficit, the reserves could be used to cover this deficit. Reserves are the net summation of all surpluses and deficits from the inception of the NPO. Reserves are very similar to retained earnings in a for-profit company. A strong balance in reserves indicates a healthy NPO and indicates an NPO with strong sustainability or a strong going concern.

## Reserves and Net Assets

We covered this briefly in an earlier chapter, but we will extrapolate on that here. Net assets are the difference from the Assets less the liabilities on the Statement of Financial Position in a nonprofit. The net assets has many similarities to equity and particularly retained earnings. The reserves are a critical component of these net assets. They can be viewed as the unused and unrestricted portion of net assets. When a nonprofit uses some of its reserves to purchase capital assets such as Land, Building, or vehicles, the reserves have been used for this but the net assets remain the same. When one buys a building from the reserves of a nonprofit for $10 M. Cash is used for that purchase, the liabilities of the nonprofit has not changed. The assets have also not changed in total value, but now instead of $10 M in cash, there is $10 M for a building. Since the assets and liabilities have not changed in value, the net assets also has not changed. Critically though, the reserves have changed. The reserves have been decreased by this purchase of capital assets. If later, we sell that building, then the proceeds can replenish the reserves.

### Depreciation and Reserves

Additionally, when we incur depreciation we are lowering our capital assets, hence, if the liabilities and overall assets have not changed, there will be no change in net assets, hence, the reserves will increase. This can be a bit complex. Imagine a nonprofit with no surplus or deficit in the year, but only had $1 M in depreciation, in order for no surplus or deficit, the nonprofit, had to have a surplus of $1 M prior to the depreciation. Hence, the net effect of this is that reserves are increased by $1 M, while the net assets remain unchanged. Therefore, depreciation can increase reserves, as long as they are not creating a deficit or increasing a deficit. If the only transaction was $1 M of depreciation and no other surplus. In this case, there would be a deficit of $1 M, the reserves would remain unchanged. The depreciation reduces your capital assets but it does not reduce your liquid assets. The deficit here only affects your net assets but not your reserves, as the full deficit was caused entirely by depreciation.

A nonprofit may decide to invest in the stock market to earn investment income, does that reduce the reserves? For the most part, the answer is no, because these investments are very liquid and can be changed back to cash very quickly. This is very different from purchasing land or a building. As well, the intention of purchasing a building is to use it for the nonprofit, not to hold it for a short period and resell.

## Reserves and Earned Income

Reserves can and should be used to generate earned income, they should also be set aside for any planned capital expenses of the nonprofit. The reserves are a good indication of the financial health of a nonprofit. The net assets is also a good indication, but if they are invested in necessary capital assets for the nonprofit, then there is far less financial stability from this class of net assets. Hence, why we focus on reserves for financial stability.

One way to understand reserves and capital assets is that purchasing capital assets will reduce reserves but not reduce net assets. Similarly when capital assets decline, such as when you amortize them, this can have the effect of increasing reserves.

A deficit that occurs during the year without it being caused by depreciation will reduce both net assets and reserves by the amount of the deficit. Hence, if we have $10 M of net assets and $3 M of reserves, then in the year we incur a deficit of $1 M, assuming no change in capital assets and no change in liabilities, this will cause a reduction of $1 M in non-capital assets, which in turn will cause a reduction in net assets and reserves. As such, our reserves will now become $2 M and our net assets will be reduced to $9 M.

## Reserves

Without a reserve, a deficit would spark a very negative reaction. This would mean that the NPO without any reserves that now has a deficit, would not have a way to properly cover that deficit. The reserves would be now in a deficit position or negative position. It would mean that the entity has more liabilities than non-capital assets. The question is who would pay for this deficit. Donors would be very reluctant to fund further, as this demonstrates poor financial management and the possibility of the entity using their funds to cover this debt. It is very difficult for a nonprofit to get a commercial loan and especially for an organization that is showing poor financial performance overall. Good governance would prevent the NPO from seeking a loan, especially one in such a dire situation. As well, it would be very unusual for a bank to give a loan to a failing nonprofit. The nonprofit may be put into a position of selling its capital assets to generate reserves, but what if these capital assets are required by the nonprofit?

Having a reserve balance in the negative is a situation you want to avoid at all costs! The effect of this situation would be quite destructive and it would likely limit how much further funding the NPO has until it can sort things out. In the case of a negative reserve, the entity is, in essence, using donor funds to fund their overall operations against what is permitted in the grant agreement. This may not be intentional but it is the only way that a negative reserve can exist. At this point, the directors of the nonprofit would need to give loans to the NPO to rectify this situation or a donor would need to agree to use their funding for this purpose temporarily. This is a situation just before a disaster, if not resolved immediately.

### Creating a Reserve or Surplus

How does an entity create a reserve? As mentioned, reserves are the summation of all the years surpluses and deficits. Surpluses add to the reserves while deficits decrease reserves. Hence, in order to create a reserve, the first step is to create a surplus for the year. A surplus can only be created through either earned income or having unrestricted funds that are allowed to be converted to surplus, above and beyond any deficit for the current year. In short, a surplus can only be created by either earned income or by unrestricted funds. A normal NPO would have anywhere from 25% to 90% of their grant revenues coming in the form of restricted grants. With restricted grants, there is no way to create a surplus. The accounting for a restricted grant is that only when the grant is expensed can the revenue be charged, hence, in this situation a restricted grant cannot create a surplus. The 15% admin fee, could potentially create a surplus but it should not. If this is done, this could create tension between the donors and the NPO. In reality, there are years where the admin fees will exceed the actual admin costs and vice-versa. Small fluctuations here will not be an issue. Hence, in one year if you have a 1% gain or a 1% loss this should not raise any concerns. It is important to keep this gain or loss to a minimum and ensure that any gains or losses can be properly treated and agreed to by the respective donor.

Hence, the two main ways to create a surplus are primarily unrestricted funding and earned revenue. Earned revenues will primarily be earned on investments, which require reserves, to begin with, but there are many other sources of earned revenues. You could sell some training services where the entity is an expert. It is important to ensure that if there is some selling of services, any costs that are funded by a grant should be covered by those fees. As an example, you do not want to sell the services of staff John Doe where he is fully paid by Donor X, without first reimbursing the grant that pays that staff. The proceeds that cover his costs should be credited to the grant and any surplus can be credited to the surplus account. This is a critical point. It is fine to credit a real profit of activities to the reserves, but one cannot do so by funding the activities by the donor and putting the revenue into reserves unless the donor is completely aware and agrees with this process. In many of these situations, the donor requires the funds to go back to the grant that earned them. This is completely reasonable from the donors and should be the expected conclusion of how a donor would prefer to treat these revenues, unless specifically told otherwise by the donor. The vast majority of times when a donor has been asked about this, they request that all revenues go back to the project. Some allow any surplus to go to reserves.

It is very unusual that a project has a net profit overall, but in some rare cases they do.

### Reserves are Difficult to Create

In short, it is very difficult to create a surplus without having unrestricted funds, as such, it is imperative to maintain a healthy balance of your reserves. Having one or two years of a deficit is fine, but this should not be ongoing and a recurring issue. Having multiple years of a deficit with no correction would be a clear indication of a going concern issue and likely indicate that some management issues need looking at. In this case, it is where the board should take an active role and demand outside help and reviews to get to the root cause of the issue.

A healthy organization should be able to build up a significant surplus over the years and this surplus should be invested wisely and should earn anywhere from 5% to 10% per year. If we look at an NPO that has an annual spend of $100 M it is ideal that 10% of this funding comes from investments, hence, if we assume that the entity can earn 10% on their investment, then the NPO should have reserves of roughly $100 M. This would lead to a very strong and stable entity. If they are managed strongly the goal would be to reduce any deficit to a minimum and increase the reserves by $10 M per year through their investment income. In less than ten years they would then have been able to grow their reserves from $100 M to $200 M.

If we look at an NPO that is fully funded through earned income. If their average earnings is 5%, they would need to have 20 times their annual spend in reserves. If we take a large organization with an annual spend of $1 B, they would need $20 B in reserves to generate the earned income to fund their annual costs. This entity does not require any donor funding at all, however, they could leverage their results further by getting additional donor funds. This leveraging could even lead to a larger surplus for them. This entity would have a large amount of costs that are funded by earned income. If they were to undertake donor projects that were partially funded by the donor and partially funded by the entity itself, this could increase the amount of surplus in the year and increase the amount of reserves ultimately. Is this strategy incorrect? Absolutely not, it is the right strategy. An NPO should be looking to protect its reserves and increase partnerships with donors. This is what every nonprofit should strive towards. It does give a bit of an advantage to those nonprofits with a higher level or earned income or a higher level of unrestricted funds, but that demonstrates that the nonprofits with a long history of positive results will benefit from that and those that do not have a long history of smart management and positive results will not benefit. Is this wrong or unfair? Absolutely not, donors should recognize nonprofits that have demonstrated results and good management. The most critical factor is the delivery of results, the NPO that has been able to generate a significant sum of reserves can only do so by generating great results or by being set up as a fund, in the first place. Those NPOs set up as a fund, must still deliver great results, if not, they will not get additional funding and will soon lose relevance, this will not be a good sign. However, most of these types of NPOs have been able to demonstrate quite strong results.

## Financial Success and Surplus

A strong surplus is akin to a strongly managed entity that is working properly and demonstrating financial integrity and prudence. If an entity has less than 5% of their expenses coming in as earned investment income, then this could be characterized as starting out or struggling. Hence an entity spending $100 M a year, should have $5 M in earned revenues if they have existed for more than twenty or thirty years. The older the NPO is, they should have a higher percentage of earned revenue. Hence, organizations that are one year old cannot expect to have a high percentage or earned income, but those over fifty years should be looking to have a minimum of 15%.

To achieve this, the starting out entity should look for a significant portion of unrestricted funding. Another approach is to have direct contributions to your fund. Many entities have used this approach and it works quite well. In essence, if the goal is to have an entity fully funded by the investment income, one could estimate the annual costs, let us assume that it is $100 M, if we are to assume 5% return, as a safe model, then one would require a $2 B investment to get this started. Many entities have been exactly started in this fashion, such as The World Bank, International Finance Corporation, Asian Development Bank, The Green Climate Fund and others. The advantage of this approach is that there is no longer a need for the entity to waste time looking for contributions each year. As well, the entity no longer is subject to significant changes in funding levels each year. This allows for a stable and more productive entity. One of the drawbacks of being fully reliant on donor funding is that in one year the funding level can change drastically which could mean a lot of new hires or a lot of laying off of staff. This is both time-consuming and destructive over the long-term.

The challenge of this approach is that it requires a large commitment upfront from each donor. This approach will take time but it is always the best approach and in the long run, will lead to better results from a donor perspective. An alternative approach would be a hybrid approach where annual funding is sought but as well, funding is sought for the fund.

Having a strong reserve balance is also a way for the entity to make capital expenditures without having to go through a donor. Capital expenditures with donors is always a tricky issue. Who owns the asset after the project? Should it be returned? Should it be sold and proceeds given to the donors? Or is it fine for the grantee to keep the assets at the end of the project? It is for these issues that often it is easier for the entity to use their reserves to accomplish the purchase of any new assets or the construction of a building. However, if there are no reserves this is not an option.

## Sustainability of the Nonprofit

The overall health of an organization can be measured in the amount of reserves that an entity has, especially when compared to the age of the entity. An entity that is 50 years old will have a great advantage to one that is only three years old. The challenge is for those long-standing NPOs that did not develop a strong reserve. This should have been put into the strategy at some point along the way and ensured that progress was made on this front. This is rarely done and often not seen as a point to consider for either the CEO nor the Board, this is wrong.

If we compare entity X and Y, one has a significant amount of unrestricted funds, while the other has a significant amount of earned income through investing in the reserve balance. Let's assume both are spending $100 M per year, but X has on average $100 M of unrestricted revenue and no other revenue and Y has $100 M of investment income and no other revenue. One may say that both are spending equally and neither are making a profit, hence both are roughly the same. There is a significant difference though. If the majority of funding is coming from one donor, what occurs if that donor decides to fund another entity or no longer can afford to fund at this level. If this occurs the vast majority of the funding will disappear. The entity has no reserves and hence will soon face serious financial issues. Entity X may see a decline in investment income in one year, this may be significant and may seriously affect the ability to match expenses with their current revenues. This would not matter, as they would have approximately 20 years worth of reserves, they could continue much as before. In the coming years, the investments will start to earn again as it is common for earnings to fluctuate, overall the future gains will offset any loss in one year. This model of relying on earned income is far safer than relying on unrestricted funding.

If there is a desire to go into a new project and close an existing project. This can be done very easily with an entity funded primarily on earned income, while this situation would be very difficult for an entity funded primarily through restricted grants. For an entity that is primarily funded through restricted grants and lacking a strong surplus, this entity will need to go to a donor and submit a new proposal to get funding before they can start the project. This will take both time and effort. This entity will be less effective for responding to immediate changes in needs.

Overall, a strong balance of reserves and where they are growing is a sign of financial strength and good management, by the same token a small and shrinking balance of reserves is a sign of weakening financial strength and could indicate poor management. If the surplus is weakening over several successive years then this is likely indicative of an internal issue more than an external factor. It is fine to have a drop over two to three years, where there are successive losses, but any more than this should be a cause of alarm for management and the board. The donors, as well, should be made aware of this. If during a five year period there is a 10% decrease in the reserve balance, while this is not a great sign it is manageable, however, if the change is a 50% reduction over five years then this is very significant and likely represents an underlying management problem that needs attention. A Board that is doing their job should not accept that five years can pass with successive losses and the reduction of 50% of the reserve has evaporated. This should call for drastic measures and perhaps an interim management team to correct the situation, if possible.

It can take decades to build up a strong reserve and a few years to wipe a significant part of it away. This is particularly true where only 5 - 10% of your revenue is derived from earned income. In this situation, it is even more critical that reserves are well guarded.

A certain minimum balance of the reserve should be set aside for close down costs. Should an entity be required to close down for one reason or another there are a host of costs that would have to be paid that are not normally accrued for. As a general rule, severance pay is not accrued for and depending on the rules this can be quite a sum. As well, there could be costs to move out or sell equipment, and returning international staff to their home base. These costs should be estimated and a minimum balance in the reserves should be set aside to cover these costs.

The financial health of a nonprofit is critical for many reasons perhaps most of all is the relationship with the donors. As an entity moves into a position of poor financial health, there is a tendency to want to show a brighter financial picture than what may be the absolute reality. This can lead an entity to get a little aggressive or creative with their accounting. These changes in accounting are not likely to be picked up by an average internal auditor until it is too late. Hence, while a worsening position does not mean that an NPO will be aggressive or creative, it is just a matter of fact that this is the only time it would be of benefit to them. Hence, a prudent donor should be more aware of a worsening financial position of an entity that they are contributing to. Also, external accountants should be that much more alert of this potential situation.

It is for this reason that the reserve position mustn't get reduced too significantly. If it is being reduced, it could very likely be moving to a place of being a permanent issue with no solution. Some situations are unavoidable like a downturn in the market, but these are usually for a relatively short period, one to two years at maximum. If it is significantly longer than that, it is likely due to poor management. The issue of poor management is caused by two groups, the management team and the board who oversees the management team. Allowing for an unstable financial situation for such a prolonged period can only be caused by poor management decision and if not corrected, this could only be made worse by a negligent and ineffective Board.

**Reserves and Financial Success**

Hence, the reserve balance is a critical measure of a nonprofits' financial sustainability and going concern. If the reserves are on the rise, this is a sign that the position is strengthening. If the reserves are significantly reduced by deficits then the financial strength is getting much weaker. If there is a sustained number of years of weakening where the reserves are significantly reduced, this is a strong indication that management is doing something wrong and as well a strong sign that the board is also not performing their responsibility correctly.

The key here is not to go from a point of relative strength to a point of relative weakness and where there is likely no turn-around possible. If the entity has suffered multiple years of deficits by the same management team and the same board, it is likely time to find a new management team and replace some key positions of the board. The concept of the same management team being able to turn the challenging environment that they have created is just hopeful thinking and a belief that can destroy a potentially good nonprofit. As well, the longer one waits to make these corrections the less likely a fix will be possible even when the right fix is implemented. The sustained neglect will result in permanent damages that will take years if not decades to correct, if correction is at all possible.

The success in sustainability of a nonprofit can only come from the success of its ability to generate impact.

# CHAPTER 18 - INVESTMENTS

"I WILL TELL YOU HOW TO BECOME RICH. CLOSE THE DOORS.
BE FEARFUL WHEN OTHERS ARE GREEDY. BE GREEDY WHEN
OTHERS ARE FEARFUL." - WARREN BUFFETT

It is very common for people to think that nonprofits should focus on delivering good or focus on delivering impact and not focus on building an investment fund. This view is based on the idea that the focus should be fully on delivering impact and this view does have some merit. However, the reality is quite different. To best deliver quality impact, the nonprofit should not have to fight for every donor dollar each year and be subject to great increases and great decreases in funding over short periods.

The best way for a nonprofit to ensure stability in funding is not only to build strong reserves but put those reserves in the safest and highest yielding investments. A term deposit or bond will not yield significant returns, but it will be very safe and stable. If the NPO puts those funds into index funds, they could earn roughly 8% - 10% per year. If they chose a stock like BRK-A or BRK-B, they could have earned even far greater. Both of these are stocks for Berkshire Hathaway, from the well known Warren Buffett.

If an NPO can generate 10% of its spending needs through

investments, then this will provide a lot of stability. If they can generate 50%, they will be that much more stable, while if they can generate 100%, they would be completely autonomous and not need to request funding each year. There are many examples of this, such as; The World Bank, International Finance Corporation, Asian Development Bank, Green Climate Fund and many others. The great advantage here is these nonprofits can focus their time fully on achieving results. They do not have to waste a lot of time fundraising and reporting on their grants. Another advantage and possibly greater, is that they do not face large changes in funding from year to year. They can ensure a stable spending rate. This would mean they do not have to constantly grow their staff and then subsequently reduce their staff size. This lack of stability causes a great cost to most nonprofits. There is a large cost to onboard a staff, to bring them up to speed, to move them from one country to another and move their family and belongings as well. Also, there is a cost to letting staff go, there are redundancy costs and relocation costs, but most importantly there is loss of knowledge and expertise.

### Increase in Efficiency

Hence, for an nonprofit to be efficient, it must have a consistent stream of earned income or a donor that has guaranteed them a significant amount of unrestricted funding. To achieve these benefits, the earned income or unrestricted income should cover a minimum of 10% of the average spend. As well, all other factors should be working. Hence, you should not be carrying any unfunded costs and your funding levels should be strong and reliable. This is the situation where an NPO can be successful. The 10% level is the minimum level, as there are certain years where funding can drop 30% or even 50%, this 10% will help but will not resolve all issues. Hence, when an entity is thriving and earning 10% in earned income, they should be aiming to get to 20% earned income levels. The minimum end goal should be 50%.

The efficiencies that will be gained by having 50% of your required revenues coming from earned income would be staggering. The focus on fund raising would still be strong but it would no longer be do or die. The NPO could focus on fewer but larger grants, thus lowering the efforts spent on fund raising and reporting. The NPO would be able to focus on projects that they feel are critical but cannot find funding for. The interesting outcome of this is that the NPO would now be very primed to attract donor funding but since they are no longer desperate for that funding, they could pick and choose the funding that is fully aligned with their goals, rather than being forced to sign an agreement because funding is at low levels.

The strong level of financial strength not only would be good for the overall efficiency and effectiveness of a nonprofit. They would not have any concerns with donor reporting. A struggling NPO, one that is facing many years of deficits in a row, may be put in a situation where they must charge an expense to a grant, even though it may not fully belong. It should never be done and it is ethically wrong to do, but with any struggling NPO, this is always a risk. This risk does not exist in NPO's that are healthy financially. As well, it is also logical to assume that an NPO that is losing their sustainability must have issues with their projects, as well. This is sort of a chicken & egg scenario. What came first the poorly executing projects or the poor financial situation.

**Vicious Cycle**
This situation can also lead in to a Catch-22 situation or if you prefer a vicious cycle. Where the poor financial situation leads to poor execution of projects and that leads to further poor financial results and so on. It is extremely difficult to recover from this sort of situation. It requires a completely different way of thinking and can only be corrected at significant cost to the NPO. Management needs to be changed, projects need to be

dropped, staff need to be somewhat changed and focus needs to be put on those projects with a positive history of results. When a for-profit company is failing, the way to fix this is to bring in new management and take some drastic steps, the same is true in the nonprofit environment.

Hence, it is critical that an NPO develops a strong reserve and aims towards 10% in earned revenue. After many decades the end goal should be roughly 25 - 50%. At this point the NPO would be very stable and able to ride any storms due to funding crises. The positive thing about having over 10% as well, is any lowering of this would be noticeable and allow for corrections to be made before it is too late. If at 5% or below, then a downturn could cause havoc without the time to recover.

At the end of the day, a nonprofit should focus on the best delivery for its recipients, but the best delivery can only come from an NPO with a strong financial base. Hence, there should be a focus on sustainability as well as impact. Investment income is needed and will help further meet the needs of the end beneficiaries. Having witnessed both scenarios, the one that has the stronger earned income has a strong competitive edge and can deliver more results to recipients. Hence, any long term strategy of an NPO should look at creating strong reserves and having a solid investment strategy.

### Is there a limit?

Can there be too much of a good thing? What if the NPO is earning 200% of their average expenses, then yes, this would not be the most efficient scenario. Once, you are earning more than 100% of your annual income, the NPO should look to increase their operations. This will deliver more impact and reduce the percentage in terms of earned income. Hence, if your average spend is $100 M per year and you start to earn $150 M per year, the NPO should look to increase their spend to the $150 M level. With the caveat that this earning is at a stable level and not due to a sudden increase in market prices.

This situation where one is earning more than their needs, is a situation that should be closely monitored so that it remains reasonable. There may be a period where the NPO is growing funds, since they are planning a significant expansion. This would be a time where it is fine to earn more than 100%, but for a limited time. This situation should also be explained in the notes to the financial statements and as well, when communicating with potential donors.

In short, any NPO that wants to focus on results and efficiency, should ensure their sustainability is in good order, by creating a significant reserve and earning investment income on that reserve. To do this correctly, it will take proper planning and decades to achieve, hence, this task must be handed from CEO to CEO and ensure that the Board is keeping a keen interest, as well. Most nonprofits do not even consider this and most nonprofits do not make any progress on this front. They are missing out on a key principle for success.

# CHAPTER 19 -
# SPECIAL REVIEWS

There are two main types of special reviews in the non-profit environment, ones that are requested by management of the NPO and those that are requested by a third party, usually a donor. Both have very different rationales and benefits.

**Internal Reviews**

The first category of reviews would come at the request of management or the board. This review is usually made to review a unit, a department, management or the CEO to determine if they are working at optimal capacity. This is usually taken on when management or the board, feels that they cannot do this review internally or through the use of their internal audit team. These types of reviews are generally requested by management with the hope of fulfilling a specific task. They would generally ask for an independent assessment of a unit. The task is generally given to a consultant or consulting firm for the review. For example, they may want to review the M&E function and may feel they need a second review from the internal auditor or a specific area to be looked at. In this case, it would have a similar function to an internal audit but would be performed externally.

These reviews if used properly can be of great benefit to

management, by providing an independent assessment of results and providing recommendations for improvement. It is important for management to review the report with the head of the unit and find ways to improve. The challenge here is that the findings may be completely different from what the annual feedback was, as such management should allow some time for the unit to address these recommendations for improvements. As well, the recommendations are just the first step, the next critical step is to get feedback from the unit head.

These types of reviews can also be ordered by the Board, this should be done when the units to be reviewed are under control by the CEO. In that case, having a review report directly or indirectly to the CEO may cause a conflict of interest. This should also be done when the report is on the effectiveness of the CEO or the Office of the CEO. As there would be a strong conflict of interest to have the report be overseen by the CEO or someone who reports to the CEO, as such the only impartial body would be the Board.

These reviews should be quite rare and only in cases where the CEO is underperforming or there is a risk of fraud. A team on the Board should be set up to determine what the consultant should review and any key performance indicators that should be reviewed. This situation should be only used where there is a problem that is persisting and the CEO does not seem capable of resolving it, such as poor fundraising or consistent deficits. Both are a sign of projects underperforming and hence poor management, each could lead to serious consequences for the NPO.

### External Reviews

The other type of review is those reviews done at the request of a third party. The third party is usually a donor but other third parties are possible. Most donor contracts allow the donor to undertake a special audit of the donor financial reports. In addition to the external audit prepared each year. This audit can be chosen on a random basis, and it is a good strategy to have both random sampling and a strategy that meets specific criteria for these special audits. Hence, if a donor has 200 grants outstanding, it may be an idea to randomly review anywhere from 2 - 10% of these per year, while also having a strategy that determines when an audit should occur. If expenses increase beyond what may be considered reasonable, then this would be a good time to initiate a specific audit. As well, these audits should be done whenever there is something does not make sense on the financial reports. One example could be that for the first nine months there is very little spend on a grant and then in the fourth quarter, there is a tremendous spend, for the NPO to catch up on their spending. There may be valid reasons for these large fluctuations but if there is no logical explanation, that is a good time to request a special audit. It is critical that this special audit report to the third party and not to the NPO, otherwise it will be of little use.

Hence, if an NPO shows a report that spends $ 5 K per month for the first nine months and then $ 500 K for the last three months. The reports should explain why this fluctuation occurred if not, the donor should request an explanation for these drastic fluctuations. If the explanations do not make sense and the general financial stability of the NPO is questionable, this is the time to have these types of audits. The goal of this type of audit is to ensure that the grant expenditures belong in this grant. The basic risk is that a grant is being charged for expenses that do not belong and are not for the benefit of that grant. To be an eligible expense of a restricted grant, four conditions should be met. The grant should allow for that cost, the cost should be directly related to that project, the project leader should approve this cost and lastly, the cost should be reasonable. The special review would be there to ensure that the NPO is not adding costs that do not belong to their project.

This is an important process to ensure that proper costs are being charged to the right places. The overall results of the M&E reports should also be reviewed along with the costs. A donor should have a decent idea of the mechanics of the M&E collection. In reality, they are receiving three reports, one is the financial report, the second is the narrative report and the final report is the M&E report. They should also have access to the audited financial statements to review. These reports should all be used in conjunction to determine whether the reports are making sense.

## Attribution of Results

One very large challenge with this is the attribution of results to specific projects. In other words, you may have two separate projects that deliver similar results. The results from different projects should not be reported in a combined fashion. To illustrate, if project A gives $5 M to get ten thousand individuals out of poverty, and project B gives $ 8 M to get twenty thousand people out of poverty. If the results of project A is nine thousand and the results of project B is twelve thousand, the results should not be combined and presented as both project A and project B getting twenty-one thousand individuals out of poverty. This could occur due to an accidental error or the way that M&E attributes the results. If this is done, then two projects that are underperforming individually can be seen as both overperforming. This is where it is important to have a full understanding of the M&E process and reporting.

## M&E should Match Costs

It is very well understood that costs should not be charged twice. There is even a term for this, it is called double-dipping. Generally, there are strong systemic rules within the ERP or financial systems that will avoid this potential error, but this does not cover all situations. A donor should understand the risks involved and the situations where these types of abnormal charging are more likely to occur. Just as charging the same expense more than once is not correct, it is logical that by the same logic, the same results should not be attributed to two separate projects. One can combine the M&E of two similar projects, but then one should also combine the costs of the two projects. In other words, if you are to include the results or impacts, you must also include those costs. The M&E should be attributed to each project only once and the whole of the organization as well.

It makes sense that the overall results compared to the costs of any given project is similar to the overall results compared to the overall costs of the NPO itself. Hence, if there is only one major impact, let us say individuals getting out of poverty. If a project has a result of $10 M spend and twenty thousand people are taken out of poverty. Then with a $100 M spend, one would assume close to two hundred thousand people would be relieved from poverty. If this value for the whole institution is only fifty thousand people out of poverty, this is a warning sign that something may be awry. If there are one hundred and fifty thousand removed from poverty, then there are likely no real issues. Your project may be performing slightly better than average, this is possible. If however, the average result is significantly lower than expected, hence, only fifty thousand, one cause of this could be the coupling of results by several projects. This may be done by error, it could be that the systems are not set up correctly or it could be aggressive measuring. This would be a situation to review, as your results seem to be way overstated when compared to average results. A donor needs to understand this issue, because, if you have an NPO with ten projects and each is $10 M per year and each shows a result of 10,000 individuals out of poverty. Then one would expect that for the whole of the NPO there would be results of 100,000 individuals out of poverty. If it is far closer to 10,000 individuals then there is a serious issue with the effectiveness of the NPO and the way the M&E is being collected and reported. It is fine to consolidate similar results, but if this is done, the costs to achieve these results should also be consolidated, if they are not presenting consolidated costs, then only the results directly attributed to that project should be shown.

It is important to understand when and how to use these special audits to ensure the reports the donors are receiving are correct, in terms of spend, the authenticity of results, and that the allocation of M&E results is done in a fair and unbiased way. If similar projects have similar results that cannot be allocated to individual projects, then two options exist, the first is jointly show those projects and report on them in totality. The other is to individually prepare the cost reports but with the M&E reports, the allocations should be done on a pro-rata basis based on costs. Hence, if thirty thousand people are removed from poverty and two projects give rise to these results, but one spends $5 M and the other $10 M, then pro-rata the results so that the first project is allocated one-third of the results and the other allocated two-thirds, which is the ratio of their spend compared to total spend.

At the end of the day, the donor must be able to be in a position to reliably understand the results of their project and the results of the overall institution as a whole. By doing so, it is the only way that a donor can know if they are receiving value for money. The donor is contributing funds to have a positive effect in a certain region for a specific cause that is of interest to them. If the reports cannot show that these results are achieved, then it will be very difficult for a donor to understand if they are making a wise investment or not.

**Transparency is Critical**
With these reports, transparency is also a key component. A donor should be able to request how the full costs are broken down by the project and how M&E results are collected and allocated, as well. However, projects and donors should remain

confidential. Donors may, and should, decide to allow their data to be shared on a confidential basis to certain or all other donors. The more donors that share their information the more complete the picture will be. This transparency will go a long way and also result in forcing an NPO to become more transparent and effective. The result will be better for the donors and better for the NPO and finally better for the most important group, the intended beneficiaries.

Ultimately, donors are providing funds to assist a group of people, the beneficiaries, to overcome a situation that alone cannot be corrected, such as poverty, hunger, disease or other issues facing this group.

# CHAPTER 20
# - OVERALL
# CONCLUSIONS

F or the nonprofit to attain success they must follow the key principles outlined in the previous chapters of this book. The most important principle is being able to deliver strong results at an efficient cost. Many elements go into this, but one of the most critical factors is the leadership of the nonprofit that is directly attributable to the CEO and the Board.

The CEO must be able to select good projects from poorly performing projects and be able to ensure that staff is properly motivated. The CEO must be able to select good staff from poor staff. The successful CEO will play a significant role in the overall efficiency of the projects within the nonprofit and hence the efficiency of the nonprofit as a whole. It is this factor that the donors will be looking toward to determine whether to fund or not to fund the nonprofit. Those nonprofits that have a history of delivering strong results will more likely get further funding and those that cannot demonstrate the ability to get strong results at efficient costs. These projects and nonprofits will not be seen as a good investment and will receive less funding.

## Improving Performance

How does a nonprofit improve its project performance? The reality is that this improvement does not come overnight. It is far easier for a nonprofit to begin to fail on this front than it is to begin to succeed, but success and improvement are possible. To improve it is critical for the nonprofit and management to figure out what is a successful project and what is not. This requires a lot of work and the ability to hear good news but more importantly to hear criticism and start to work at that. Often the nonprofits that can hear constructive criticism are the ones that require it the least and the ones that cannot listen to constructive criticism are the ones that require it the most, the same is true of the leaders of these nonprofits. The leaders that are the worst performers are the ones that need to take the most criticism and act on that but are also the least receptive to constructive criticism. This leaves the nonprofit in very poor shape. This is why often when it rains it pours.

Another critical principle of success for a nonprofit is the financial health of the nonprofit. The interesting aspect is that the better the first principle of success, then also the second most important principle, its sustainability is more likely to be successful. However, for this second principle to be highly successful, it requires strong financial leadership and a CEO who understands the importance of this. It requires a strong CFO who is given a green light from the CEO to ensure the financial health is critical. This is particularly important when the financial health of the organization is already unstable. The priority would be to get the nonprofit in a financially sustainable shape, the CEO must also be on board with this priority, if not, then the nonprofit will not take the necessary steps to get into financial health. This will also cause major problems for the organization as the reserves of the organization will become more depleted as it sustains further deficits and the financial situation gets worse each year. On the other hand, a strong CEO will work closely with the CFO and focus on this priority, together and over a year or two the financial health of the organization can be restored and while this is going on, they can focus on improving the efficiency of their projects.

## Yin and Yang - Impact and Sustainability

The impact or doing good of the nonprofit and its sustainability are its yin and yang, respectively, and the two most critical principles for success. Having one alone without the other will lead to failure. A highly successful nonprofit will need to balance both the impact and its sustainability. To manage sustainability, one must manage risk, it is not to say the nonprofit cannot take any risk, but they should only take calculated risks and only risks that they can afford to lose.

The projects are an important component of the nonprofit and in reality, the nonprofit is the summation of its projects. Hence, it is an important principle to be able to manage good projects and to be able to properly monitor the progress on projects. Being able to know which projects are performing well and which projects are poorly performing is vital to success. The nonprofit must know which projects are delivering well and which are not. The ability to discern this difference is why a strong M&E team and function are important. Many nonprofits do not put enough emphasis on this aspect, while it is a very important function. Imagine a company selling smartphones but not being able to tell which phones function well and which do not. They would not be able to determine which product lines should be dropped and which ones should be ramped up. They may spend a lot of money trying to sell poor products to the public. In a nonprofit, there is a lot of funding going towards delivering output, but there is only a small fraction of that cost that evaluates whether that impact is being delivered efficiently. The nonprofits that excel and put the proper efforts towards M&E activities will have a large advantage over those that do not.

The issue is that when funding falls or the financial health begins to struggle, the last team to get additional resources is the M&E team. Often, the M&E function is performed by individuals with very little real education or experience with M&E. Perhaps they took a course or a class on the topic, but very few have relevant expertise in this field. Some nonprofits put the proper importance here but even with that being true, the M&E function, on the whole, has many challenges. The first challenge is the attribution of results, we can measure results but can we attribute those results to that project? This is a key issue. The other issue is the results of M&E usually have a long list of impacts and outcomes, but these are very difficult to put monetary values on, as such, they cannot be added together. If we have 100 different measurement items, we can summarize that list to 100 but we cannot add them together. Imagine on our balance sheet, if instead of showing our Supplies as $15,000, we showed 10,000 sheets of paper, 1,000 pens, 200 toners, etc. The advantage in finance is that we can summarize these items by monetizing them, we are not there yet in terms of M&E. Although many people intrinsically can put a range of values for a given output, there is no formula for doing so. These two issues make M&E that much more difficult, but it does not mean that it should be avoided. Most nonprofits have their project teams do the bulk of the work of M&E and sometimes this work is overseen by a person with some knowledge of M&E. The problem here is that the people measuring the results should be independent of the project, but in most cases, they are not. While M&E is a very important factor, very few get this one right. Some are on the right path but even many of those are far away from doing it fully correctly.

The final key principle for a successful nonprofit is the staff members. It is critical to have the right talent mix. The successful nonprofit will be able to attract the strongest staff there is but also able to retain these staff members and ensure that they are properly motivated. Motivation is often not emphasized enough, but having the best team around that is not properly motivated compared to having a strong team that is properly motivated, the properly motivated team will outperform the stronger team by having the right motivation in place. The nonprofit must be able to attract, retain, and motivate its staff members.

The nonprofit that can ensure projects are delivering strongly, ensures a healthy sustainability, has great teams in place, properly motivates its staff, and is taking the proper efforts with regards to M&E will be one that is also highly successful.

# THANKS TO YOU

I would like to thank you so much for reading my book.

It is my priviledge to be able to present these ideas to you. If one nonprofit is able to better help one beneficiary, then the book can be considered successful.

Again, thanks for your time, and appreciation!

As well, I would like to thank my endless supply of coffee, this book would never have been completed without my four or five cups daily!

As well, after many rounds of edits, there are still corrections and improvements, thanks for understanding that a few may have slipped past.

We would love to hear any feedback from you - please click here to do so

# BOOKS BY THIS AUTHOR

Money Matters for Personal Finance

No matter your financial situation - improve it!
This book will show you how to save on your costs, maximize your revenues and get the most out of your portfolios. We will show you how to invest your money to have a safe portfolio but yet very well-performing. These techniques beat out 90% of very well-paid Wall Street broker

# ACKNOWLEDGEMENT

I would like to thank my peers, my colleagues, my friends, my family, my supervisors, my staff and all who supported me throughout these years. Without your support, this book would never have been written.

# ABOUT THE AUTHOR

## Mark Gruner

He is a professional financial accountant and adviser, with experience working on four continents with international organizations. He has worked as Chief Financial Officer and most recently as Director of Finance. Mark studied at McGill University first doing a Bachelor of Science in Biochemistry. He later moved into the field of business and did his graduate degree in Public Accounting. After that he went on to become a Chartered Accountant.

His first work was with a small audit firm, he then moved to Coopers & Lybrand. He moved up the ladder quickly but felt that he did not have a passion for audit. He decided to work overseas in finance. He began his first overseas job in Sarajevo, Bosnia working with International Rescue Committee. He then took the role of Chief Financial Officer for a Dayton Peace Accord Organization named, "The Commission for Real Property Claims for Displaced Persons and Refugees (CRPC). Before taking on this role, the organization was struggling and did not have proper accounting systems in place. Within a very short time, he turned that situation around for the positive and the organization began to thrive. This organization had a fixed mandate to decide on the vast number of property claims for displaced individuals. In the final year of operations, CRPC had decided all the claims that were possible, the remaining claims could not be decided due to lack of evidence. It was then closed down.

While CRPC was closing down, Mark took on another role in Sarajevo with International Finance Corporation, part of the

World Bank Group. He was hired as the Senior Resource Management Officer (SRMO). He was put in charge of Finance, Information Technology, Human Resources, Administration, Metrics & Evaluation, and Logistics. He performed very well at this job and was given a promotion to work in Istanbul, Turkey to cover the Region of Central Asia as the Regional Financial Controller. He performed this job very well and earned a performance award, an award that is presented to a small handful of people per year at International Finance Corporation, he had earned two of these awards in two years.

After about five years of working for IFC in the Balkans and Central Asia, he had decided that his team was now strong enough and he was ready to move on. He was given the choice of two jobs in a short period, he chose the most challenging one. That was the job of Regional Financial Controller for Africa. At the time, this region was struggling in terms of finance. It had a history of poor internal control results for its country offices, was poor on budgeting/forecasting and reporting, it was also struggling with issues in procurement. This would be no easy task. Within two years, Mark had moved the team from the worst region in terms of financial controls to one of the best regions. He had put in policies to improve the forecasting and budgeting procedures and revamped the reporting process. This led to an improvement, and Africa became one of the best. The Vice President of the region, commented, that since we have made these improvements, he no longer worries about the financial reporting. He now only spends one or two percent of his time concerned with that area. He compared himself to others who spend twenty or twenty-five percent of their time focused on financial matters.

Most recently, Mark Gruner worked as Director of Finance for International Rice Research Institute. He came to an organization that was struggling. The funding had dropped dramatically in 2016 and with no solution in sight was headed for a large deficit of about $10 M, roughly 10% of their revenue. With some quick planning and cooperation from all teams, he had implemented a plan where they would be able to save approximately $ 8 M in one year. This plan was executed and the organization was able to continue to thrive.

Mark has now gone on to pursue his passion for writing. He continues to work as a consultant and entrepreneur. You may find more about him by visiting his website at MarkGruner.com

# GET IN TOUCH WITH THE AUTHOR

Visit the Author's Site: *https://markgruner.com/*

Visit Author's Site on Amazon:
*https://www.amazon.com/Mark-Gruner/e/B081JMM152*

Submit a question or feedback:
*https://markgruner.com/contact-us/feedback/*

Join the Author Facebook page:
*https://www.facebook.com/Mark-Gruner-100249968345613*

Interested in being a beta reader or alpha reader? Contact us.

Contact Green Bridge Consulting to have a discussion about improving your nonprofit :

*https://greenbridgeco.com/contact-us/*

www.ingramcontent.com/pod-product-compliance
Lightning Source LLC
Chambersburg PA
CBHW021405210526
45463CB00001B/228